Jeanne Chilton

"Soul Searching"

The True Nature of Ghosts, Demons, and Paranormal Phenomenon

Series

Book 1

Copyright 2013 Jeanne Chilton

All Rights Reserved. No part of this book may be reproduced or transmitted in any form or by any means without permission of the author.

Title ID: 4481590

ISBN-13: 978-1492980483

Create Space Publishing

Dedication

To my beloved Grandma, Daphna Craft

It is not goodbye. It is just so long until we meet again.

Just remember, I'll be here until the very end.

I may be gone, but you should know, I have been here from the start.

And, even though you can't see me, you will feel me in your heart.

It is not goodbye. It is the test of time that strengthens us within.

Until the day that our souls are free to meet up once again.

It is not good bye, remember me in every moment given.

And, keep with you my promises to be with you in heaven.

Written by Jeanne Chilton for Daphna Craft at age 12

Acknowledgements

I would like to thank many individuals for helping me to make this book possible.

My Grandma, Daphna Craft for her unconditional love and understanding. Her strong spiritual belief and peaceful presence that has been a guiding light in my life. Her protective spirit and everlasting impression upon my life that has led me on this journey.

My Father, Leon Rudolph, who is one of the most selfless people I know. Thank you for always pushing me to believe in myself. Your love has given me great hope when I didn't believe it was possible. Your strength has instilled in me the desire to do what is right and never forget God is guiding our hand in everything we do.

My friends and family for always seeing me for who I am and encouraging me to follow my own path no matter what others would say. I appreciate your long hours of listening and enduring my many theories and research observations.

Thank you for standing by me through all of the emotional ups and downs. I will always cherish your constant love and support of me.

My close friend Dale Kaczmarek who has provided much knowledge and expertise in the field of paranormal research.

My close friend Mike McElhiney who has stood by me, supported me, and travelled long distances to assist me in my search.

Lastly, thank you to all of those who refused to listen to me when I sought answers to my experiences; who rejected my questions and told me I was going to hell; who told me I would confuse others. If it had not been for the rejection and close mindedness, I may have accepted your beliefs and not followed the path that led me to the truth.

Table of Contents

Introduction--8

1. Why My Search Began the Night She Died---------------14
2. How Our Beliefs Are Formed------------------------------29
3. Common Beliefs About Ghosts----------------------------45
4. History of Ghosts and Demons----------------------------58
5. What Does the Bible Say About Ghosts-------------------68
6. What Does the Bible Say Happens When We Die--------83
7. What Does the Bible Say About Other Phenomenon--99
8. Analyzing the Information--------------------------------120
9. Revelations and Consequences---------------------------134
10. True Stories of Demonic Possessions--------------------150
11. Why the Church Does Not Talk About It---------------168
12. What It All Means---------------------------------------180

Glossary of Terms--190

Sources--201

Notes---204

"The eyes ... are the windows of the soul.
~Plato 427 BC

Introduction

In this book, we will address some very hard questions concerning religious/spiritual belief, supernatural forces, ghosts, demons, angels, etc. Whether you have been afraid or ashamed to ask specific questions regarding the mysteries that surround us, we must accept the fact that there may be things beyond our mind's comprehension that do in fact exist. I urge you not to accept anything that I am telling you in these pages, but use the information I have provided to search for the answers yourself. I only hope to help lead you to the correct source to find the answers to your own questions. I will take you on the journey I have travelled to assist you in finding the answers to these plaguing questions that many of us have asked ourselves. We will explore this road together in a search for answers, meaning, and truth.

Whether or not you believe in the existence of life after death, angels and demons, ghosts and God, most individuals need to find meaning in their purpose while living, and search for the reasoning for it at all. Most of us desire to know if there truly is life after death and if so, where do we go? Many of the questions, I will address in this book, may be questions that you have asked yourself or pondered over in order to feel a sense of peace within your life.

My hope in writing this book is to open your mind and free yourself of any preconceived notions in order to truly re-evaluate the information. When we begin with a clean slate, we can look with fresh eyes and see things from a totally different viewpoint. This book will not only open your mind to the possibilities of the existence of the supernatural, but open your hearts to the real truths in order to find peace within yourself.

When selecting my title, I searched long and hard within myself to find the perfect representation of the meaning of this book. While laying wide awake as I often do, the title came to me "Soul Searching". This title has multiple meanings to me which is ironic due to the fact that this book has the same.

First, it represents my passion as a paranormal researcher to explore and document the existence of supernatural forces in order to understand my own experiences. Secondly, it represents the ability to search within ourselves (our souls) to find meaning and understanding in our lives and personal experiences. Lastly, it connects my soul to something much greater than myself.

I would like to start by saying, though we may all have a different opinion of the issues addressed in this book, I respect each and every opinion given. Our beliefs are formed from our upbringing, faith, teachings, and personal experiences, which makes each and every one of them valid. Reality is what is real to you. Our realities may be similar or different, but valid just the same.

My intent in writing this book is not to convince or persuade anyone to become a believer in ghosts/spirits, and supernatural forces, but open your minds to the possibilities that have been given to us to test and explore. I hope that when you read this, you will be able to relate your own experiences whether personal or supernatural to the foundation of this book.

I have spent my whole life searching for answers to things I have experienced. In my search for the truth, the road has led me to writing this book and discovering information well beyond what I ever thought. I will share my findings with you and let you be the judge of what the truth is.

I can tell you that probably every one of you that reads this at some point in your life, has tried to find meaning or searched within yourself for what your purpose is.

We will take this journey together to search for the answers to questions, we have asked, wondered about, or been given answers that do not fit our reality as we know it to be. Many will disagree with me and that is ok. Our differences are what make us who we are. Wouldn't life be a boring place if everyone thought the same way? Would we ever have anything new to learn if we never challenged our minds and beliefs?

We will analyze these questions by addressing the information we have been given to study. These areas include culture, religion, psychology, science, academia, history, archaeology, paranormal research, and many others. I will also be sharing some of my own paranormal and personal experiences that have led me on this path in search of truth. I will provide as much factual evidence as possible to allow you the ability to research the information and back up my beliefs. I will also provide resources for you to begin your own personal search.

Much of what I will tell you will sound quite extraordinary. I can only tell you, my hand to God, that the experiences I share with you is my reality. This information will be considered controversial by some and heretic by others. My goal is not to deceive, but provide the truths behind these mysteries, why we experience things in different ways, why our questions go unanswered, and what to expect in the future. I only ask that you continue to read forming your own opinions as you go.

Chapter 1

Why My Search Began the Night She Died

I will begin by describing one of the most influential people in my life and then take you back to the night in October of 1983 when all of this began for me. My Grandma was the most special person in my life. She was my protector, my security blanket, my best friend, and the most Christian woman I have ever known. I remember her presence like that of a calm and peaceful quiet. There was an energy about her that radiated deep into my being. Whenever she was around, I felt love like most people never experience. She would tell us bible stories as we sat on the floor. Playing her guitar, she would sing praise to God. She was one of the most loyal Christians always praying for those in need. She thoroughly studied many different religious texts and denominations. Her search for truth would be limited in those days to lack of resources. With very little education, she began her own self-study. The knowledge and wisdom she possessed would come by her very desire to ask God for assistance.

I would sit at her feet or up in her lap listening attentively to everything she had to say; absorbing all of the knowledge she possessed and shared with me. I remember her standing in front of me, so I would not be punished. I remember her holding me and the security I felt in her arms. She would tell me things that I did not understand at the time, but later have come to understand. She told me I was special and to use my gifts. As a small child, you listen not always understanding the deeper meanings until one day, you remember and it all makes sense.

Her strong presence commanded attention, though her approach was peaceful and calm. She had a way of drawing you in close to her without ever asking. Her spirit was pure and her mind open. Her search was guided by light and love. Her teachings were simple, yet contained so much knowledge. One day her search would be cut short.

My Grandma had been very ill from diabetes. She was bedridden for some time. Although, I remember her being sick, most of my memories are from the time she was not. She had a stroke and was hospitalized for many days. She was paralyzed on one side and unable to walk. She began to show signs of improvement. I was hopeful that she would recover. I remember hearing the family talking of a particular day when she said the Lord was coming for her. Did she know she was leaving this earthly plain? Was she preparing the family for her departure?

Then in the early morning hours of October 17, 1983 something extraordinary and devastating happened.

My little sister 6 years old and myself 8 years old at the time were sleeping on the bottom bunk together when around 3:00 am in the morning she awoke and had to use the restroom. She walked down the steps into my mother and father's room. She opened the door to the bathroom and as she flipped on the light, I saw two large figures standing on both sides of the toilet (I have illustrated what I saw below).

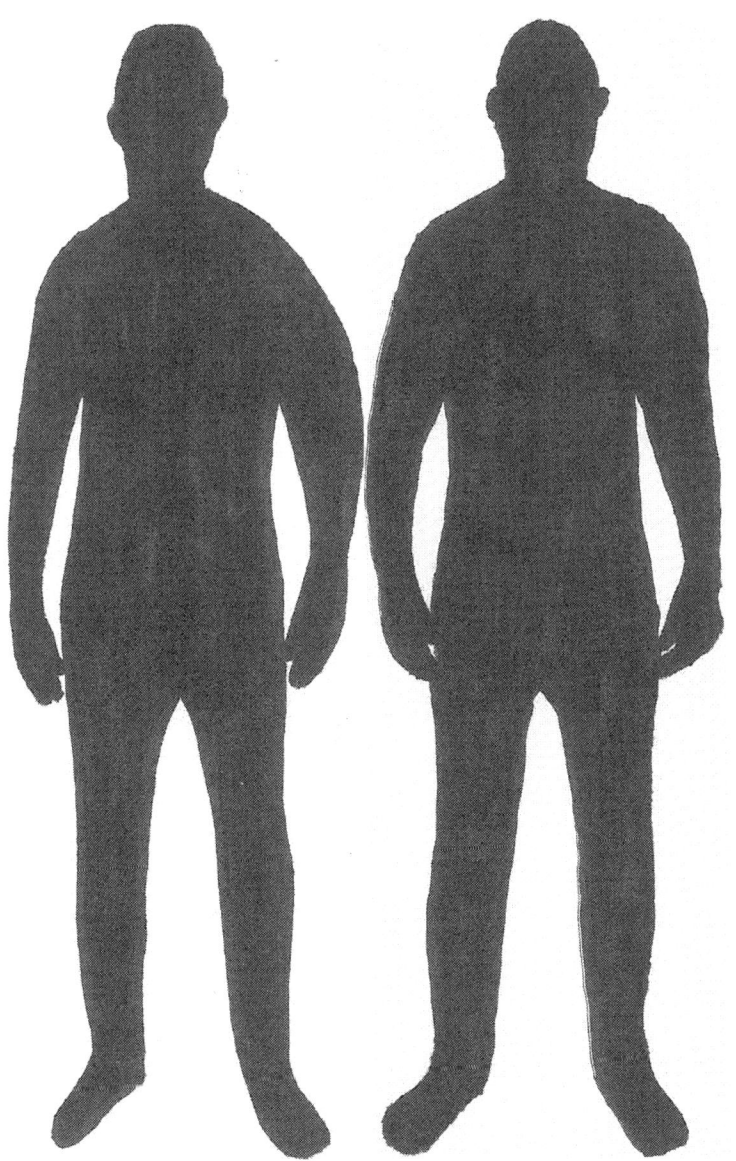

There was no motion, no features, just still darkness of what were tall men. I blinked my eyes and when I opened them the door was shut. Seconds later, my sister ran out of the bathroom crying, waking my parents and telling them, there were two men in black in the bathroom. My parents rushed to the bathroom and there was nothing there. They calmed us down and went back to bed. A couple of hours later, the call came from the hospital. She had passed, but was on life support until the family could get there.

I will never forget the deep sorrow I felt that day. The emptiness and sadness that can only be explained as a deep hole in my soul. The fear of what I had seen kept creeping its way into my mind. The question of what could it be would follow me to this very day. The significance of it, I would not know until much later in life.

This would be the first of many experiences that would follow me through adulthood. However, this particular experience has been the driving force in my life ever since. From this experience, a flood of uncertainties arose. Questions that I can only describe as driving me to find the answer behind the mystery. What did I see? Why did I see it? What did it mean? I had to know.

I remember talking to the pastor, family and friends. Asking questions which no one had the answers for. Being told I was going to hell by religious believers when I would question their statements about the non-existence of these things. Their interpretation that it was a dream or could only be a demon sent to deceive me. I became withdrawn, more frightened, and considered the odd one. I often wondered, was I bad? Was I evil? Yet somehow, no matter how bad I felt, I could still feel her loving, embracing spirit around me. That same peaceful energy surrounding me telling me it would be ok. Was she still protecting me? Was it her or something else? I always knew deep down that the lasting impression she had made on me, I would someday leave for others as well. I would follow in her footsteps to be the very best person I could be. The same selfless, loving person; caring for others without a thought of the same in return.

After a little time, I began to experience other things. Some of these experiences were terrifying, while others brought a sense of peace. They were always different. There was no consistency, no answers, just more confusion, more questions, and more fear.

One night while sleeping, I awoke to the covers over my head. I was kicking and fighting trying to get them off, but they would not budge. I was screaming and crying, terrified and uncertain of what was happening to me. The next thing I remember, I saw the light come on through the covers and my mother pulled the blankets off of me. To this day, I am claustrophobic. I cannot sit against a wall or sleep on the side of the bed closest to it.

I would dream things sometimes and then they would happen. I would get images of a person I had never seen in my head and then it would disappear. I would feel something around me when nothing was there. I would be close to someone who was upset and seem to feel the very same thing they were feeling.

For a long time, I kept all of these secrets to myself. Then later there was only one person who I felt I could talk to, my daddy. He became the same loving security that she once was. I only confided in my father for fear of ridicule and being made to feel as if I were strange. He would listen, but never pass judgment. He would protect me from those who treated me differently. He did not understand, but accepted me for who I was.

I was treated differently and made fun of by the kids at school. I didn't fit in. I was awkward, shy, and very self-conscience. I had a hard time trusting others and would keep to myself mostly. I was different than my sisters. I always felt the need to question everything. I could never just accept what I was being told. This was especially the case when it didn't fit what I knew to be true. I had to see it with my own eyes in order to accept it. I had to research it further until the truth could be found. I would get sentences in school for asking too many questions and challenging the responses I received. Coming from an old fashioned family, this got me in a world of trouble. A child is to talk only when spoken to, and it was never ok to question an adult.

Then for a few years, it seemed as though whatever was happening to me had stopped. The next experience would come at the age of 12 years old. My father bought us a new house. My mother went to paint and we came along. My little sister and I running around looking at all the new exciting rooms. We ran down the stairs and when we got to the bottom, we both froze in fear. We felt like there was a woman down there, although we didn't see anything. We ran screaming back upstairs to my mother telling her someone was in the house. She went and checked and of course there was nothing there. We got in a lot of trouble that day for scaring her.

My sisters and I began to experience strange things in the house. We would see shadows pass down the hall when no one was there. Alarm clocks would go off that were not set. Car alarms would sound for no apparent reason. I always felt like someone was watching me in my room. And then one day, while cutting the grass on the riding lawn mower, a ball of light appeared in front of me. It was the size of a beach ball, Yet the colors within it were changing constantly as if it were electric, morphing internally. It floated slowly passed me as I watched it disappear into the trees. We began to hear footsteps in the house. Objects would disappear and reappear months later in plain sight. These were just a few of the oddities we were experiencing in the house. My father kept telling us it was our imagination and that nothing was there. Over the course of years, there were many different experiences. Sometimes, there would be long periods of time in between, but they never stopped happening for me. The most significant experience for me was the night she died. I could never forget it; those two figures standing in still darkness, watching me and projecting an energy which is hard to explain. There was something about the mystery of what I saw that had to be solved.

From 8 years old until I was 35 years old, this question had never been far from my thoughts. I pondered over it daily, trying to understand. Doesn't the darkness represent evil? It instilled fear in me. It produced a constant uncertainty and questioning of everything I had ever been taught. I questioned religion, I questioned God, and I questioned everything. I was terrified of death. I could not approach a coffin for fear of seeing them again. This made no sense to me as my Grandma was a beautiful, god loving person inside and out. What did it represent, and where would I find the answers I was seeking?

Many questions about the experiences plagued me. Why was I different? Why did I see and feel things no one else could? What was so special about me, and what were these gifts my

Grandma told me to use? With all of the questions and uncertainties, I decided to go my own route in search of these answers. No one could help me, no one understood, and no one had the answers I sought. I was told the bible didn't speak of these things because if God did not tell us about them, they didn't exist. At the age of 35 is when my paranormal search began.

Some close friends of mine had started their own paranormal group. I decided to tag along on an investigation one day and see what it was all about. From that day forward, I knew somehow through this research, I would find the answers. I began contacting local sites to ask permission to do investigations. Amazingly, I found it was quite easy to get approval. I began doing many investigations and it snowballed from there.

Shortly after I began, I was contacted by numerous people wanting to join the team. I formed my team and began to document the existence of paranormal phenomenon. As I became more familiar with different types of equipment, searched histories of locations, and analyzed my findings, I now knew, I wasn't crazy and these things are very real. I would not understand until much later, the journey that these experiences and information would take me on. This would become a venture far beyond the existence of ghosts.

I will be sharing more of my experiences with you in other chapters of this book. Each of these have significance in the different areas of research I have been led to. The experiences and evidence that I have captured put me on a path to discover things I believe have been long forgotten and in some cases deliberately hidden from us, most of which is quite incredible to say the least.

One of the main questions when I decided to go into this field was, are ghosts the souls of people who have lived and died, or is this some other dimension that sometimes is able to cross into our world and reveal itself to very few? Through different evidence I had captured and experiences I was still having, questions would soon begin to reveal themselves as a road to the answers I had longed to find.

Let me say that the desire to search the paranormal field was never about the thrill as you see it on television. It was never about the excitement of experiencing a ghost. It was however about finding the truth behind my experiences and sharing it with others to educate them about what was truly going on. If I could help one person to overcome the fear of their frightening experiences and help them understand, then I had accomplished what I had set out to do. I have met many respectable people along the way. Many of these individuals are some of my closest friends. I have formed relationships and have earned respect in the paranormal community. There is a right way and a wrong way to do things. The right way will lead you to the answers. The wrong way could leave you wishing you had never let your curiosity get the best of you.

I urge anyone who is interested in getting into the paranormal field to be careful. What you are looking for, you just might find and it may be more than you can handle.

In a day and age where we are being desensitized to the phenomenon through radio, movies, and television, it is important to understand that in reality, this is not a show. It is not glamorous. It is dangerous and you can be affected negatively; though it is made to look exciting and in every episode you can expect to either see or hear a ghost.

I can tell you from experience it is nothing like what you will see in a 30 to 60 minute episode. The things you seek may very well follow you home and disrupt your life as well as others lives in ways you could never imagine. On the other hand, the questions you seek to answer can be answered by asking the right person. I will explain who that is in another chapter of this book. If I had never taken this path, I would still be pondering over those same questions. The answers would never have been revealed to me, and the publishing of this book would never have been made possible.

Chapter 2

How Our Beliefs Are Formed

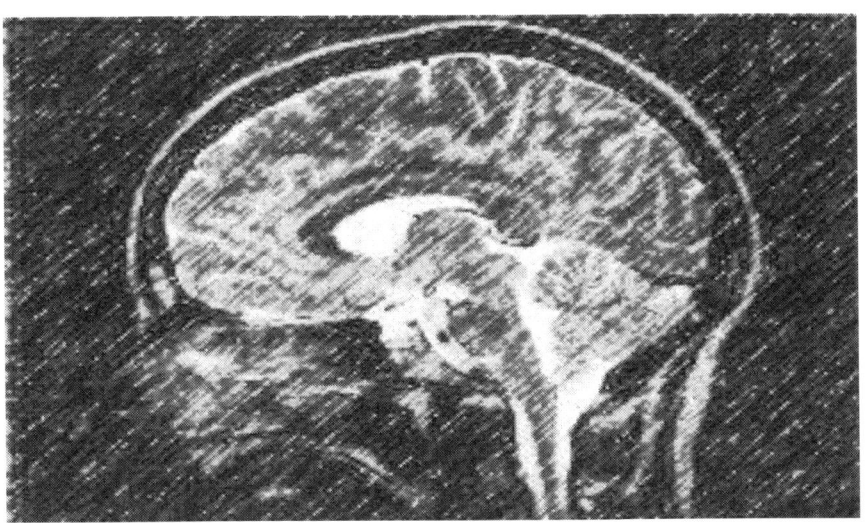

In the previous chapter, I began to explain to you how from a very young age, I knew I was different. Let me stress that I do not feel that I am psychic, nor do I believe that I am any more special than anyone else. I do understand however, that I see and feel things differently than what is considered normal in our society. I believe that each and every one of us has been given gifts to serve different purposes. The bible itself with all of its mysterious wonders, tells us the same.

1 Corinthians 12:7-10

Now to each one the manifestation of the Spirit is given for the common good. To one there is given through the Spirit the message of wisdom, to another the message of knowledge by means of the same Spirit, to another faith by the same Spirit, to another gifts of healing by that one spirit, to another miraculous powers, to another prophecy, to another distinguishing between spirits.

In this chapter, I will show you how I began to understand and embrace my differences. This will be important to each of you as well, in understanding how we begin to believe, what we each personally value, and why those beliefs form our very being and reality.

The desire to understand who we are and the purpose we serve can only be explained once we have been given the tools to decipher it. Our personalities are all different. This has been studied thoroughly in psychology leading scientists to believe that the basic structures of our personality and formed beliefs are different across cultural variations. The concept of personality explains the commonalities in individual behavior over time and during exposure to certain situations. Persuasion involves the communication of arguments and information for the purpose of changing one's beliefs. This can be found in every area of our lives whether from society, family, religion, culture, or experience. Persuasion can be easily accomplished if the person communicating the information has high credibility. This would include expertise and trustworthiness. Likability also plays a key role. If we like someone, we tend to focus our attention to listening to what they have to say. Beliefs are the feelings an individual has about people, objects, and ideas. These beliefs are thoughts and judgments that we apply to these specific areas. In order to persuade someone to acceptance of certain beliefs, we must understand how this process works. The following model of the persuasion process is provided due to extensive research in the field of psychology. There are many source factors that allow for someone's beliefs to be altered.

Overview of the Persuasion Process

Who	What	What Means	To Whom
Source	Message	Channel	Receiver
Credibility Expertise Trustworthy Likability Attractiveness Similarity	Fear appeal verses logic One-sided versus two-sided argument Repetition	In person On television Via audio Via Internet	Personality Expectations Preexisting beliefs

Persuasion of our beliefs can be considered a form of abuse. Let me explain further. The process of persuasion via means of propaganda can discourage careful reasoning and scrutiny. In many ways our beliefs can be forced upon us and if not accepted there are consequences applied.

When you were a child, you were given certain ideals to accept and adhere to. Your beliefs in many ways were taught to you by the expectations of your parents or the religion you were raised with. For fear of punishment, you accepted these rules and followed them.

Example: *You are raised in the Baptist religion. You are told that the catholic religion is evil and you are never to set foot in a catholic church. If you do, you are going against God and will surely go to hell for accepting these false teachings.*

Now, to a young child, this is a very scary thought. Who wants to burn for eternity? This fear caused you to accept the belief that the Catholic religion is evil. You then grow up and begin to teach your children the same lesson. The pattern continues. If we look at this logically, is it true that everyone who is Catholic is evil? This is very unlikely. However, the strong belief has been instilled in you and for fear of consequences you close your mind to any other interpretation. Belief is the strongest aspect of our lives. We will begin to discuss how our beliefs are formed, and how these very beliefs can keep us from understanding, seeing, and finding the truth. We must learn to look outside of our preconditioned beliefs in order to find the truth. By closing our minds to other ideas and only looking at one side of thought, we will always arrive at the same conclusion whether it is true or false. Understanding this type of logic will be critical in allowing yourselves the ability to look at the information with an open mind. The journey I will take you on to search for the answers to your own questions will only be successful if we rid ourselves of false teachings.

One day at work, I received an email that all employees were to attend a two day mandatory training session that weekend. I grumbled and complained. Who wants to give up their weekend to sit in an all-day training? Understanding the blessing of having a job in this day and age, I stopped complaining and accepted I would have to attend.

Saturday morning came. I went to work finding my assigned seat and hoping the day would go by fast. As the training began, I realized this was not a typical workshop. This was about something that would help me discover the significance of my differences. It would open my mind to understanding the road I was being led on to discover the truth and answer the questions I was so desperately seeking.

As the training began, we were told that we would be learning about how our attitudes create our reality. This was expressed in a scenario that when we focus our attention in a certain direction, we can create the result we do not want to happen.

***Scenario:** You are walking in a big open field. There is nothing around except a single rock. You begin looking at the rock telling yourself to avoid it. Your mind is so focused on the rock that you begin to veer in its exact direction causing you to stumble and fall.*

The goal of this exercise was to show us by simply changing the way we think, we can create a different result. If we focus our mind on the big open field, we avoid the rock keeping on the path we choose. We avoid the obstacles that stand in our way of what we are searching for. Have you ever had anything like this happen to you? I can tell you, everyone in the room broke out in laughter, because we could relate a personal situation or hurdle in our life to that rock. Have you ever heard the saying, "You did this to yourself?"

Next, we began to talk about our beliefs, and how these beliefs influence our lives. First, we were to determine how each of our beliefs were formed. The study of Psychology has proven that there are certain key factors in the forming of our beliefs.

1. Culture-Religious or Social
2. Environment
3. Experiences

I want each of you to think about one thing you believe in strongly. Now, I want you to think of how you came to believe that way. Was it something you were taught in church, home, or school or did you experience it? Was the belief influenced by one or all the factors listed? Now let us examine a belief from two viewpoints that we can each relate to. God exists verses God does not exist.

To the believer, there is no question that God exists. He is influencing every aspect of their life. He gives blessings for leading a Christian life and brings hardship punishing those who live a sinful one. He allows Satan to influence us. Only by praying, repenting, and accepting him will we one day receive eternal life.

To the unbeliever, there could not be a God. What God who is supposed to be so loving would allow for such pain and suffering of those he created? Who would allow innocent children to be molested and animals to be harmed? Why doesn't he show himself or answer our prayers when we ask? Why doesn't he lead us to the truths instead of keeping us confused and questioning everything?

No matter which belief you have, I am sure that you feel very strongly that your belief is the right one. How was that belief influenced? Were you raised in church or in a family of non-believers? Were you taught he exists or is non-existent? Have you experienced the power of prayer or been left with unanswered ones?

As you can see from these analogies, our belief about his existence is valid for each individual no matter what side of thought you're on. But how do we begin to justify our beliefs with fact and truth. And, how do we begin to unravel the mystery surrounding it? We will analyze this further as we continue.

In the next portion of my training, we were told to watch a video. I ask you to stop reading for a moment and watch the video for yourself. Follow the instructions exactly as they are stated.

Here is the link http://youtu.be/vJG698U2Mvo

If the link becomes unavailable, please search "Selective Attention Test" and watch the video.

STOP! Do not look at the next page until the exercise is complete.

DID YOU LOOK AT THE PAGE WITHOUT WATCHING THE VIDEO? I TOLD YOU NOT TOO. DID YOU FOCUS ON THE ROCK INSTEAD OF THE FIELD? YOU JUST STUMBLED. NOW GO BACK AND WATCH THE VIDEO.

If you did the right thing, turn the page and keep reading. Congratulations! You will now be able to understand the purpose of this exercise.

Now that you have done the exercise, be completely honest. Did you see the gorilla? If you have done this exercise before, did you see it the first time? 95 percent of individuals do not, while 5 percent do. How could this be possible? How could you not see something the size of a person right in front of your face or how did you see something no one else could? In the remainder of this chapter, I will explain the significance of this exercise and how important it will be for you to understand your beliefs and change your way of thinking. That is when your journey will begin in finding answers to your questions.

In the proven science and study of Psychology, people begin to develop at a very early age mental scotoma's. This according to Psychology is a figurative blind spot in a person's psychological awareness. The individual is unable to gain insight into and to understand. What this means, is that we develop mental blocks. These blocks keep us from accepting and even seeing things that are right in front of us.

We reject what does not fit our current beliefs, we focus our attention to what we have been told to do. We reject those things that don't have meaning for us. Like robots, we are preconditioned to see only what our beliefs or instructions will allow us too. Therefore, our minds block information and physical reality from our existence. Challenging our beliefs, causes mental conflict. When we go against what we hold to be true, this challenges our current understanding of what we personally believe. We then begin to convince ourselves that there is no conflict by rejecting the information, avoiding the topic, or explaining it away as if it is false.

For the few that saw the gorilla, you may be one of the 5 percent. I can almost bet, if you saw the gorilla, you have had a paranormal experience at some point in your life yourself. I was the one in the room who saw the gorilla that day. This would come as such a startling revelation for me. The significance of seeing the gorilla would forever change me. I now understood why I was different. I now understood why I could see things others could not. I now understood my desire to question and analyze everything in search of the truth; my inability to accept without further study what others told me. I left that day with a sense of empowerment. Understanding if, I could clear any remaining scotoma's and open my mind, I could then begin to find answers and understanding to what I had experienced from a very young age.

I encourage you. Do not abandon your beliefs, but remove what you have been taught to believe. If you do not do this, you will only try to make every experience fit your current accepted belief. These scotomas will keep you from finding the truth. Once you let go, you will begin to see things much more clearly. You will begin to re-evaluate everything you have been taught and see a different story unfolding.

In the remaining chapters, I will begin to share more of my paranormal experiences which has led me to researching a wide range of areas. I will reveal who and where the answers came from and where you can find them as well.

Chapter 3

Common Beliefs About Ghosts

Now, knowing why I saw things, I then focused my attention to the questions of: What was I seeing and what did it mean? I now understood why some individuals are able to see them and others are not. With one question answered a door was closed. Now another door opened to continue my search. This began my journey to unlock the mystery and decipher the true nature of ghosts. Are they the spirits of the dead? Are they angels and demons? Is it another realm that crosses our path?

Additionally, there are many other paranormal occurrences that do not fit in with our current belief of what a ghost is. How do we begin to find meaning in these experiences as well?

The history of ghosts reaches far back into antiquity. From the earliest of civilizations in Mesopotamia to the modern times, people have reported seeing and being frightened of them. Different cultures and beliefs have formed over time as to what the nature of a ghost is. Many believe they are angry spirits or demons. Others believe they are the souls of people who have passed away. They are referred to by different names in a range of cultures such as Shiryo, Jinn, Aojha, Bhoot or Bhut.

The most widely accepted belief, is ghosts are the spirits of a person who has passed. Many of the reports describe particular locations that contain trapped spirits due to tragedy. Others report visions from fully solid figures to mists that appear to dissipate. There are also various descriptions about types of hauntings. I will describe a few of the most commonly reported hauntings.

A traditional haunting is considered to be a spiritual entity is aware of the living world and interacts with or responds to it. These are also known as intelligent hauntings. A residual haunting is described by many to be repeated playbacks of

Sensory phenomenon that is attributed to a traumatic event. This has been described as a replaying of events. Demonic hauntings are believed by many to be supernatural, malevolent forces. The belief in demonic hauntings can be traced to most religions, cultures, occult practices, and folk lore. Demons are said to have the ability to possess living people resulting in negative thoughts and actions. They can move objects and cause harm to the living.

Although, there are many others that have not been listed here, these are the most widely reported and accepted beliefs. I have already shared with you, I became a paranormal researcher. During my investigations and continued study, I had captured much evidence to support that ghosts/spirits are in fact a very real phenomenon. Why some people experience them and others do not, I now knew.

Evidence that has been captured includes audio, video, and photographic. I will share some of the photographic evidence with you.

Captured by Michael Chilton (Figure of a woman)

Investigation at a hospital. While doing a walk-through of the facility, the image on the left hand side of the photo was captured.

Captured by Jacob Bizaillian (Shadow appeared)

An individual claimed her leg was very cold. When a photo was taken, this was captured. Notice how it is formed at the base of her foot.

Captured by Rita Doe (Shadow figure of a child)

Photo snapped when someone said they were seeing shadows. Look at the doorway. There is a dark figure the size of a child.

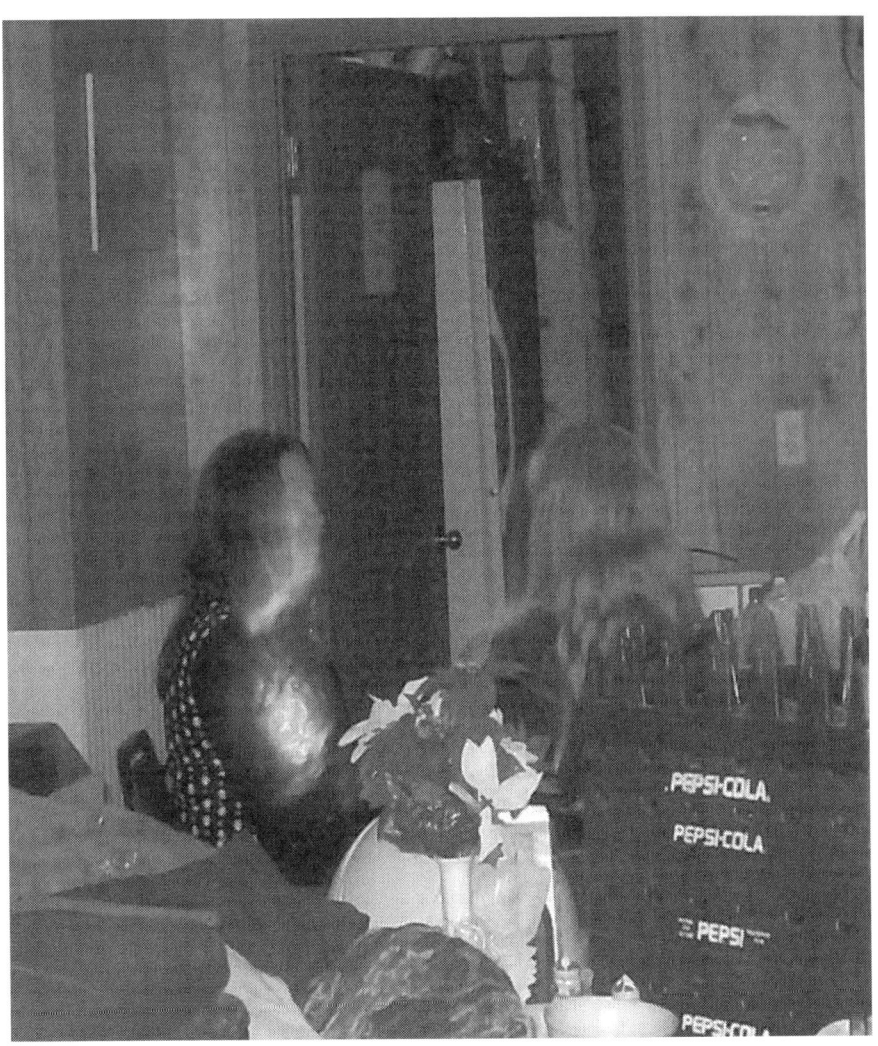

Captured by Theresa Moore (Skeletal hand on face)

An individual in the photograph stated it felt as if someone was touching her back. A photo was taken, and what appears to be a bony hand on her cheek, a glowing light on her chest, and face behind her is captured.

Captured by Jeanne Chilton (Figure in the doorway)

While taking photographs in my building for the insurance company, this image was captured in the doorway right in front of me.

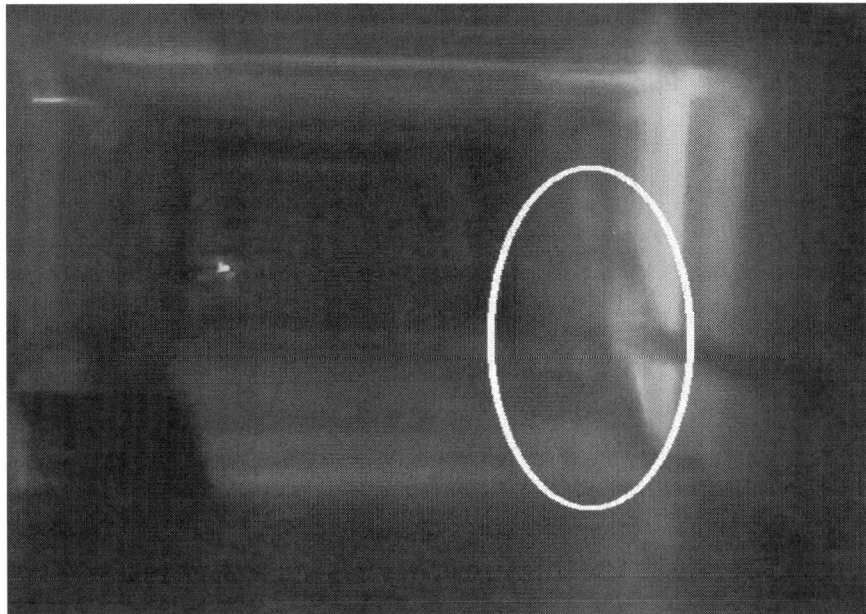

Captured by Jeanne Chilton

A figure holding the handrail

I assure you each of these photos is authentic. One thing my paranormal colleagues have learned about me is, I get very upset at the idea of fake evidence. I have no desire to become the next big show. What purpose would this serve other than trying to get ones name out there? I am an honest person, sincere in trying to help others and find the truth behind the experiences many of us face. In order to gain respect in the field, we must only provide sound evidence. We must only do this with the intent of exposing the truth and helping others find answers to their questions. In order to educate others we must disclose both our research findings and the dangers involved in seeking this knowledge. My decision to search for the answers by doing paranormal investigations rather than seeking out the answers from the appropriate person has not come without a price. I will go into this much further in the book with you.

I began to look at the evidence I had captured on investigations. I played back in my mind the situations and circumstances when the evidence was captured. My belief in ghosts was only further validated by these findings. Having many discussions with fellow investigators on the topic, it seemed as though the questions just led us in circles. After all, why is it that the responses we seem to receive never fully answer the questions asked? In fact, the lack of a definitive answer leads one to ask more and more questions, drawing you in further. If these are the spirits of loved ones or people who have passed, and they have the ability to respond with a one word answer, wouldn't they also have the ability to come straight out and give a definite answer to the question?

Then there are those that say they have seen a loved one after they have passed. This brought a sense of peace to them. Others explain frightening experiences without understanding of why these things are happening to them. Further in this book we will begin to analyze these very situations and find meaning.

These varying accounts of paranormal phenomenon do not fit

into one category, but fall into different categories as I will begin to show you. Our beliefs about the existence or non-existence of these phenomena can be changed if we begin to listen openly to what others are saying.

You yourself may not have ever had a paranormal experience, therefore the belief has not been instilled in you. For those that have, the need and drive to find answers to these mysteries keeps you searching to find the truth. If you continue to read this book, I think you will find that from either perspective, your eyes will be opened to new found knowledge. I have delved into the mystery so deep that I believe I am qualified to lead you to where you can find the answers. You will not find them by asking the ghosts to respond to your questions. You will not find them by listening to what others opinions are on the subject. You will not find them by rejecting the teacher who is trying to reveal it, and you will not find it unless you research and test everything you have been told to believe.

It is my intention to lead you to the place where these truths are revealed; to the place you were told you wouldn't find them; to the place that others who study it have been blinded to seeing and hearing the message they too are supposed to receive.

If we continue to only look at one side of the story, we will always end up with the same result. The same biased knowledge we **BELIEVE** to be true.

In the remaining chapters, we will begin to analyze these questions and our current understanding of the nature of paranormal phenomenon. Whether you are a believer or unbeliever, I feel that each of you will find that you will learn something new outside of your current world view on the subject. We will search and test every aspect to find truth.

Chapter 4

History of Ghosts and Demons

In this chapter, we will begin to look at where the first accounts of ghosts and demons stem from. This will be crucial to understanding how our beliefs have evolved over time. I have done much research on this topic. I have traced the belief to the earliest of civilizations.

Let me begin with our current understanding and belief. We will then begin to go backwards in time, tracing these beliefs until we end up at the first cultural and religious reports. Today, ghost stories and experiences have become dinner conversation. More and more individuals are sharing their experiences publicly and openly. What once was considered a taboo subject has become a worldwide socially acceptable phenomenon. Almost every channel you turn to, has a show regarding ghosts, demons, mediums and psychics. The media has made this phenomenon popular.

It is a source of entertainment for most people. Christians and non-Christians alike are being captured by the media. This does however diminish the serious nature and desensitize most individuals to the understanding and danger associated with seeking knowledge into these things. The popularity of the supernatural has led curiosity seekers to trespass on private properties trying to find and experience a ghost. Hundreds of paranormal teams have formed just in the last couple of years. Many of these teams simply looking for an adrenaline rush, while others are seeking truth and knowledge in order to help others and understand their own experiences. Television does not prepare you for the amount of knowledge and understanding needed to be successful in this field. There are many physical and spiritual dangers that come with paranormal investigation.

Many investigators go into a location and begin to cuss and provoke to get a response. Let's say that our belief is true and ghosts are the spirits of our loved ones passed. How disrespectful is it to go into someone's home and cuss at them, telling them to come out. If I was a ghost, I surely would not show hospitality to these individuals. This is to show the type of ignorance and disrespect many of these new teams possess. Their lack of knowledge and lack of moral values is surely going to put them in an undesirable situation.

The current beliefs of many individuals are that ghosts are the deceased who have somehow remained attached to certain locations and individuals and in some cases objects due to sudden death. On the other side of this, there are those who believe that there are only demons who are seeking us out in order to deceive us and lead us astray.

Many locations are often associated with traumatic events that have led to a haunting by these deceased spirits. It is believed that these spirits are trapped in these locations being forced to relive the tragedy again and again. Not all locations are associated with a tragic event. There are many cultures that believe the essence of a person continues to exist where their energy and memories are powerful.

20 years ago, you did not hear about ghosts other than sitting by a campfire telling ghost stories. Though the stories have been passed down from generation to generation, they were mostly attributed to folklore, myth, and for the mere purpose of trying to scare one another with the exception of those who have had personal experiences.

The fear of being ridiculed or labeled as evil kept many from sharing these experiences or asking questions.

In the middle ages of medieval Europe ghosts were typically classified under two categories. There were souls of those who have passed and demons. The only time the soul of a loved one would return was for a specific purpose. Demons are not considered to be an existing soul of a deceased person. Their sole purpose was to deceive and lead the living astray from God. The belief further stated if an individual were to demand to know the purpose in the name of Christ, the deceased soul would explain their purpose, while the demon would be cast away.

The ancient Romans believed a ghost could come seeking revenge towards their enemies. They could carve a curse into pottery and then place it into the grave. A Christian priest, Constantius of Lyon recorded a continuous theme of ghosts coming back to haunt the living in the 5th century AD. This would continue until the bones had been discovered and a proper burial performed.

In Greek mythology, the Khu, was seen as a malevolent spirit or ghost who can enter living bodies and torture them. This ghost (Khu) was also referenced in ancient Egypt, but in this case was considered to be the soul, or voluminous part of a human. When separated from the physical body, the Khu (soul) was released, but remained somehow in the physical world.

This same belief changed in later Egyptian times to the Ba, which was then considered a direct descendent. Over a time period exceeding 2,500 years, Egyptian beliefs evolved continuously. These beliefs can be found in artistic paintings, scrolls, and inscriptions. You can find many of these beliefs in the Egyptian Book of the Dead. This contains the belief about ghosts and the afterlife from different periods of time in their history. You can purchase this book from Amazon by going to www.amazon.com and typing the title in the search bar. The earliest civilization known to man, were the Sumerians. In Mesopotamian religions of Sumer, Babylon, Assyria and others, ghosts were believed to be created at the very moment of death. At this moment they would descend to the netherworld and lived in a separate realm comparable to the living. Relatives were conditioned to make offerings and sacrifices in order to avoid misfortune and disease. Some of these diseases and illnesses were also thought to be the work of God's and demons.

In the Hindu culture, a Bhoot or Bhut is a supernatural creature. This is usually referred to as the ghost of an individual who has passed away. The ideas of how these creatures came to exist varies in different regions. They are considered to be restless spirits, due to some type of sudden or traumatic death that prevents them from moving on to the other side. Bhoot's are believed to be able to take on different forms either animal or human.

Additionally, there are many religious beliefs containing references to ghosts, demons, and occult practices. There are some Christian denomination's teachings that ghosts go to a middle state (purgatory) where they remain before continuing on their journey. Most Jewish and Christian teachings are consistent that attempting to speak to or conjure spirits is sinful and can lead to contact with demons. The purpose of these unclean spirits to deceive and draw people away from God.

The belief that the spirit manifests into a ghost after death is a widespread idealism. As I have shown, these stories have been passed down from the very first civilization in Mesopotamia. This puts the dating on this belief back to the time when ancestor worship was taking place.

Ancestor worship included religious practices, funeral rites, exorcisms, and also cases of ritual magic and sorcery. These practices were performed to put the spirits of the dead to rest. The practice of ancestor worship was primarily to keep vengeful spirits away from the living.

The practice of sorcery was also very common in these cultures. Many believe they could contact the dead and even bring them back to life through ritualistic ceremonies. Ritualistic practices would be carried out to communicate and bring up the spirit of their ancestors who were linked to the God's.

In ancient times, the first ancestors were believed to be directly descended from the Gods. Some of these ancestors were considered half or three forths divine. In a search for immortality, many occult practices became common.

No matter which culture or religion we study, the common emotion associated with a ghost, spirit, or demon is that of fear. This fear is associated with the unknown. Our inability to understand the true nature of ghosts, and the varying beliefs, cause confusion and disruptiveness in our minds. These ghosts are not a natural state of being and their purpose unknown. The automatic reaction to experiencing this phenomenon is usually fear and uncertainty.

Now, after following this information to the earliest of sources, we are still plagued with what the real nature of ghosts and paranormal phenomenon are. As you can see, from culture to culture, from then until now, the varying beliefs and interpretations still leave us with the same unanswered questions. What we can see from this, is that paranormal research has not definitively identified and solved the mystery. The ancient and historical records have not proven what the true nature of a ghost is. Individual interpretations vary from person to person. Cultural and religious belief also have varying and changing ideas. So where do we find the truth?

As, I pondered over this question, I had to turn my search to the only source I knew of that could clear up the mystery. So far, not one individual had a definitive answer. Not one source had led me to conclusive understanding. I would turn my search to the source I was told didn't contain the information. The Bible.

Chapter 5

What Does the Bible Say About Ghosts?

I ask you, if you are a believer in God to look at the information I will be providing in the next few chapters with an open mind. Read the verses for what they are saying, not what you have been told they mean. For the unbeliever in God, I ask that you read these as well, looking at them from the perspective of a history lesson. Many of the events of prophecy in the bible have already taken place. Many of the locations mentioned in the bible have been found through archeological excavation. This tells us the words contained within are based on truth and not myth as many believe. The purpose of my research is to analyze every viewpoint and every source of information to arrive at the truths. We cannot and will not find the answers until we identify how these views began. The confusion will continue until we put our preconditioned ideals aside and look at each side of the information.

I have already shown you, that in every culture and religion since the earliest of times, ghosts and demons have been reported. Though, the stories vary from source to source, this tells us this was happening and interpreted differently depending on who was telling the story. If everyone from the beginning believed in their existence, shouldn't we also believe there has to be some truth to it? It is not simply based on false teachings or myth, but taken from the stories of individuals who were seeing and experiencing it.

I began to read and find specific verses that spoke of ghost/spirits. I find it hard to believe that some Religious individuals do not accept that the paranormal/spiritual phenomenon is very real. The bible is filled with verse after verse of supernatural and mystical happenings. Some do believe these things are real, but explain it away to only demons. Do you believe in demons and angels? Do you believe that Christ rose from the dead? Do you believe individuals received messages in dreams and visions? If you said yes, then you believe in paranormal phenomenon. Why couldn't these experiences that many of us face, also fall under the category of angels, messengers, or visions rather than demons? In some of these instances, could they not also be positive experiences or messages leading us to seek truth? It is possible that in these experiences an individuals scotoma's keep them from being able to decipher the messages sent to them. I can tell you in my experience, it was 35+ years before I would begin to decipher the message.

If you have been led away from God because of having experiences that did not match the church teachings, you will find in this chapter that you can find your answers to these mysterious questions in the biblical text. No matter which side of thought you are on, we can begin to examine these questions from a single source. At that point it will lead you to other sources of information.

What does the Bible Say about Spirits/Ghosts? Some of you

may have wondered about this question, while others may have actually asked it to someone such as a family member or pastor. Many of us have wondered if the bible does indeed speak of spirits/ghosts. I personally have asked this question many times. The responses, I have received have been inconsistent and confusing at most.

While some might say the bible does not speak of these things, because they do not exist, others say if there is a reference in the bible regarding this question, it has been misinterpreted by the reader. So I ask, who is misinterpreting it? The person who knows ghosts/spirits exist by the very experience of seeing them, or the ones who accept their non-existence purely by their own preconditioned belief. I have been told by many religious believers that there are only angels and demons. I have been told by these same individuals as well as others, I will go to hell for searching for the answers to this mystery. So, there is one person I can rely on that lets me know if what I am doing is wrong.

In my search for the answer to this question, I have determined that I could not find the answer by asking someone who does not have it. I turned my focus to the place I believe these answers could be found.

1 John 4:1-3

Dear friends, do not believe every spirit, but test the spirits to see whether they are from God, because many false prophets have gone out into the world. This is how you can recognize the Spirit of God: Every spirit that acknowledges that Jesus Christ has come in the flesh is from God, but every spirit that does not acknowledge Jesus is not from God.

I believe we are being told to test these things. Whether visible or invisible, there are powerful forces at work. I encourage you to look at the verses I am about to provide to you and make your own interpretation of God's word.

Matthew 17: 1-3

And after six days Jesus took with him Peter and James, and John his brother, and led them up a high mountain by themselves. And he was transfigured before them, and his face shone like the sun, and his clothes became white as light. And behold, there appeared to them Moses and Elijah, talking with him.

Moses and Elijah who have long been passed and taken appear in front of these men. They would be classified as a ghost under our current understanding.

Verse 9 goes on to tell us:

and as they were coming down from the mountain, Jesus charged them saying, tell the vision to no one until the son of man has been raised from the dead.

Jesus tells them not to tell anyone until he is resurrected. This was a very real phenomenon that took place that day. They were only to reveal it, once he himself became like them. The soul transformed into a vision and shown to many in illuminated form.

Matthew 14:26

*But when the disciples saw him walking on the sea, they were terrified, and said, "It is a **ghost**!" and they cried out in fear.*

Mark 6:49-50

But when they saw him walking on the lake, they thought he was a ghost. They cried out, because they all saw him and were terrified. Immediately, he spoke to them and said, "Take courage! It is I. Don't be afraid.

Luke 24:39

*See my hands and my feet, that it is I myself. Touch me, and see. For a **spirit** does not have flesh and bones as you see that I have."*

Depending on the version of the bible you're reading, these words will change between spirit and ghost. The disciples specifically reference a ghost as being the spirit of someone they know. Though, Jesus was not deceased at this point, the disciples truly believed they were seeing his ghost. What is important to point out here is Jesus does not tell the disciples a ghost does not exist. He tells them they do not have flesh and bones as they see he does. Now, knowing what I do about biblical teachings, Jesus would not have allowed his disciples to continue believing in something that was non-existent. He curbs there fears by explaining that he is flesh and not a spirit.

Mark 16:12

After these things he appeared in another form to two of them, as they were walking into the country.

Jesus takes on an unrecognizable form. This would coincide with some of the ancient beliefs about spirits having the ability to change form. Jesus as well as many other verses in the bible speaks of occasions where men are seen in a different form.

Matthew 27:52-53

The tombs also were opened. And many bodies of the saints who had fallen asleep were raised, and coming out of the tombs after his resurrection they went into the holy city and appeared to many.

Bodies of the saints were resurrected after Jesus. They were seen by many. The souls of these saints were also raised and reunited with a bodily form appearing to many. I will explain later how they did not ascend to heaven, but returned to their earthly grave until the appropriate time.

Matthew 27:50

And when Jesus had cried out again in a loud voice, he gave up his spirit.

At the very moment of Jesus's death, his spirit leaves the physical body. In other versions of the biblical text, this word is exchanged for the word ghost. We are being told, at the moment his last breath leaves him, his spirit/ghost separates from the physical body.

1 Samuel 28:11-15

Then the woman asked, "Whom shall I bring up for you?" "Bring up Samuel" he said. When the woman saw Samuel, she cried out at the top of her voice and said to Saul, "Why have you deceived me? You are Saul!" The king said to her, "Don't be afraid. What do you see?" The women said, "I see a spirit coming up out of the ground."

The ghost/spirit of Samuel is brought up after death. This is performed by a medium. I will expand on this verse in chapter 8.

What we can see from these verses is that ghosts/spirits were in fact a belief even in Jesus's day. The bible tells us that these things were seen and understood even in those times. The verses I have provided are not referring to demons, but of what we call ghosts today. The spirits of those who have passed.

In the case of Elijah, we are only told that he was taken in a world wind so that he would not see death.

Revelations 20:14

Then Death and Hades were thrown into the lake of fire. This is the second death, the lake of fire.

It is also quite possible that he was transfigured into a spiritual form when he was taken. We know that Moses was buried by God, so his body would not be found. This would explain why Elijah was shown alongside Moses and they both were speaking to Jesus. We are not being told this is an angel or a demon. We are being told specifically, Jesus, Elijah, Moses, Samuel and the bodies of saints were in fact seen after their death. In some of these instances, I have shown that not all of them were ghosts, but the resurrected bodies in the flesh of those who have died and were reunited with a physical body or shown in glorious splendor. Some other verses show resurrection as well.

Luke 8: 52-55

Meanwhile, all the people were wailing and mourning for her. "Stop wailing," Jesus said. "She is not dead but asleep." They laughed at him, knowing that she was dead. But he took her by the hand and said, "My child, get up!" Her spirit returned, and at once she stood up.

John 11: 38-44

Jesus, once more deeply moved, came to the tomb. It was a cave with a stone laid across the entrance. "Take away the stone," he said. "But, Lord," said Martha, the sister of the dead man, "by this time there is a bad odor, for he has been there four days." Then Jesus said, "Did I not tell you that if you believe, you will see the glory of God?" So they took away the stone. Then Jesus looked up and said, "Father, I thank you that you have heard me. I knew that you always hear me, but I said this for the benefit of the people standing here, that they may believe that you sent me." When he had said this, Jesus called in a loud voice, "Lazarus, come out!" The dead man came out, his hands and feet wrapped with strips of linen, and a cloth around his face. Jesus said to them, "Take off the grave clothes and let him go."

Luke 7: 11-15

Soon afterward, Jesus went to a town called Nain, and his disciples and a large crowd went along with him. As he approached the town gate, a dead person was being carried out – the only son of his mother, and she was a widow. And a large crowd from the town was with her. When the Lord saw her, his heart went out to her and he said, "Don't cry." Then he went up and touched the bier they were carrying him on, and the beurers stood still. He said, "Young man, I say to you, get up!" The dead man sat up and began to talk, and Jesus gave him back to his mother.

Acts 20: 12

On the first day of the week we came together to break bread. Paul spoke to the people and, because he intended to leave the next day, kept on talking until midnight. There were many lamps in the upstairs room where we were meeting. Seated in a window was a young man named Eutychus, who was sinking into a deep sleep as Paul talked on and on. When he was sound asleep, he fell to the ground from the third story and was picked up dead. Paul went down, threw himself on the young man and put his arms around him. "Don't be alarmed," he said. "He's alive!" Then he went upstairs again and broke bread and ate. After talking until daylight, he left. The people took the young man home alive and were greatly comforted.

Resurrection takes place when the soul is reunited with the physical body. The spark of life returned. Through these many verses we are being shown that the spirit/ghost is separate from the physical body. The physical body ceases to function while the spirit goes on.

Are you still confused? Is this question still unanswered? The Bible does in fact speak of spirits/ghosts. Many will say these verses speak of demons or angels. My question to you is, if that is in fact the case, why are demons and angels referenced throughout the Bible, while these specific verses reference ghosts and the individual names of those who had passed away or were taken by God specifically? Does that not tell us they are different? Have I not shown you with God's words that these are not instances of angels and demons? We have to look at the deeper meaning behind these situations. It is clear from the biblical writings each one of these instances are for the purpose of delivering a message to all those who saw. But, there are also very valuable clues that lead us to the truths behind them. We will begin to analyze these verses further in Chapter 8.

This does not however, stop our search for these answers to other phenomenon. This does not explain all of the various reported experiences that people have been encountering since the earliest of times. It does however tell us that there are differences between ghosts, demons, and angels in the biblical text.

1 Corinthians 15:44-46

It is sown a natural body, it is raised a spiritual body. If there is a natural body, there is also a spiritual body. So it is written: "The first man Adam became a living being"; the last Adam, a life-giving spirit. The spiritual did not come first, but the natural, and after that the spiritual.

In the next chapter we will begin to explore other paranormal phenomenon found in the bible. If you're not convinced these answers can be found here, keep reading and watch the mystery unfold.

Chapter 6

What Does the Bible Say Happens When We Die?

Now, I would like to look at another question most of us can relate to. One of the questions, I feel each and every one of us has asked is, "What happens to us when we die"? We have often wondered if we do go to a better place or cease to exist. We will start by looking at what the bible says about this question. Some of you have been taught we go straight to heaven or hell. Others are taught we go to purgatory until we are able to move on to the next level. Some believe we are asleep until the judgment day and others believe it is the end of our existence.

From my research, I fully understand that many of the experiences people have do not include seeing someone familiar. In some cases, people have reported seeing a loved one, etc. Was this truly their loved one, or something familiar sent to bring peace and understanding? So how do we begin to understand these experiences and their meanings? Many reports of paranormal activity involve objects moving, apparitions, dark shadows, electrical malfunctions, etc. In these instances we can say for sure from the verses given in chapter 5, we are not having the experience of seeing a ghost of someone who has passed.

I have already shown you where many of these beliefs come from. Many of them have been passed down since the earliest of times, others taught to us by church and family. Now let us look at what the bible actually tells us is happening.

What Happens When We Die

John 3:13

No one has ascended into heaven except he who descended from heaven, the Son of Man.

Hebrews 9:27

And just as it is appointed for man to die once, and after that comes judgment

Genesis 3:19

By the sweat of your face you shall eat bread, till you return to the ground, for out of it you were taken; for you are dust, and to dust you shall return."

Ecclesiastes 9:5

For the living know that they will die, but the dead know nothing, and they have no more reward, for the memory of them is forgotten.

Psalm 146:4

When his breath departs, he returns to the earth; on that very day his plans perish.

1 Thessalonians 4:13

But we do not want you to be uninformed, brothers, about those who are asleep, that you may not grieve as others do who have no hope.

Ecclesiastes 12:7

And the dust returns to the earth as it was, and the spirit returns to God who gave it.

Psalm 104:29

When you hide your face, they are dismayed; when you take away their breath, they die and return to their dust.

Job 34:15

All flesh would perish together, and man would return to dust.

Psalm 115:17

The dead do not praise the Lord, nor do any who go down into silence.

Job 14:12

So a man lies down and rises not again; till the heavens are no more he will not awake or be roused out of his sleep.

1 Thessalonians 4:16

For the Lord himself will descend from heaven with a cry of command, with the voice of an archangel, and with the sound of the trumpet of God. And the dead in Christ will rise first.

Daniel 12:2

And many of those who sleep in the dust of the earth shall awake, some to everlasting life, and some to shame and everlasting contempt.

2 Corinthians 5:8

Yes, we are of good courage, and we would rather be away from the body and at home with the Lord.

Revelation 20:5

The rest of the dead did not come to life until the thousand years were ended. This is the first resurrection.

John 6:44

No one can come to me unless the Father who sent me draws him. And I will raise him up on the last day.

Ecclesiastes 3:20

All go to one place. All are from the dust, and to dust all return.

In these verses, we are being told, the body returns to dust. All dead, either good or evil goes to the same place. The dust. The dead can no longer have any part in the affairs of the living. It is not until the judgement day when Christ returns, those who are asleep will be taken with those in Christ who are still alive. We will then be raised from the dead. Now, if this doesn't happen until a future event takes place, one might ask, "Then where do we go?

In science, we are taught the energy cannot be created or destroyed. It is always present. From my healthcare background and my many years of study relating to the heart and the human body, this scientific theory is correct. Our hearts produce electrical impulses and without the spark of energy, it ceases to beat and all function stops.

Normal Heart Beat (Life)

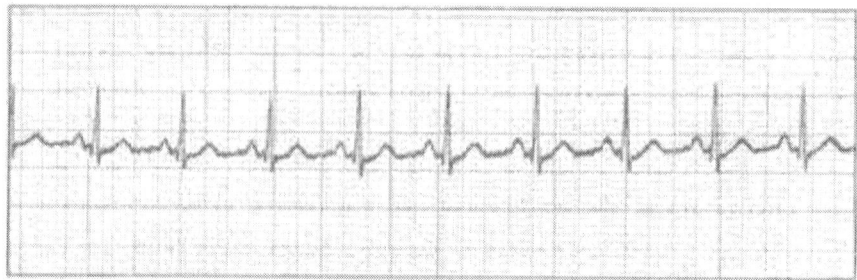

Flat Line/Asystole (Death)

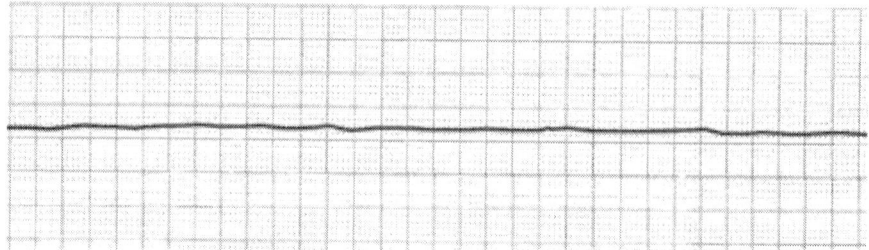

This electrical activity is measured to capture these impulses. Additionally, our bodies contain static charges. You experience this with goose bumps when you are subjected to fear or cold. Have you ever seen a spark produced when you touch a doorknob? This is also a form of static electricity.

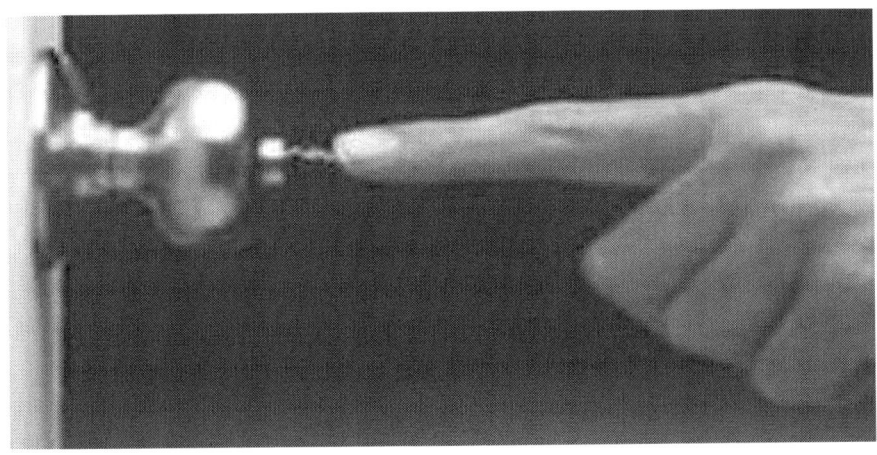

(Maher Science, 2010)

All living creatures produce energy. This is proven and documented through many years of scientific and medical research. If this energy leaves the body at the moment of death and cannot be destroyed then where does it go?

If we look closely at the biblical text, we are told in fact that our souls will return to the body in the resurrection. This is telling us that our spirit does not die, but the physical body does. Our soul does not go directly to heaven instead it is held in a dormant state until the time it is reunited.

A bear hibernates in the winter. Falling into a deep sleep, it remains in this state until spring arrives and it awakens. This is a natural process by which the bodies function slows down and is in a dormant state until the appropriate time.

Is it possible that our souls remain in this same dormant state until the appropriate time? According to the text, there are only certain times when the soul of a loved one is allowed to come forward. The spirit of life is then reanimated into the vision or physical body of this loved one who has passed. This is only at the will of God.

We can see these same miracles happening today. However, they are not in a mystical sense. In these same verses I have shown you in the previous chapter, not only Christ, but also his disciples were given the power to resurrect to life certain individuals. I believe that today, we are given those same powers. Let me explain.

We have talked about times when resurrection took place. Either by the hand of Christ or through his will individuals were given power to bring the dead to life. With the abilities, knowledge and technologies available to us today, we also have this same ability.

Working in the cardiac intensive care unit for many years, I would see many individuals both young and old having massive heart attacks. When a patient would code, we would run to the room and begin administering CPR. Once the defibrillator became available, a shock of electricity would be sent through the patient's body. Sometimes this would restore life and other times had no effect.

I would watch as two patients with the same condition one at the age 26 would not make it while the other at age 77 would live. Is this not at God's will? Only he has the power to control when it is our time to go.

Flat Line/Asystole (Death) to restored Normal Heart Beat (Life)

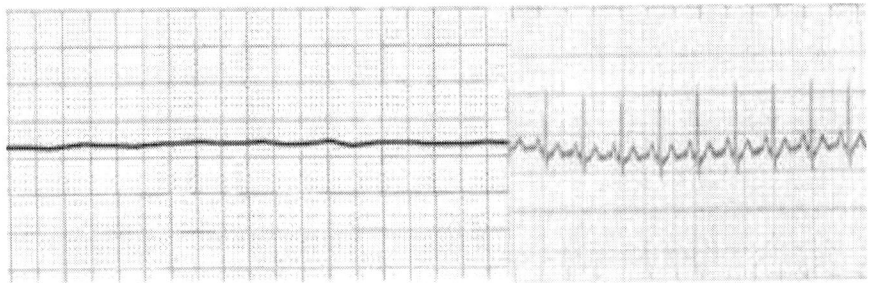

Are we not being given the same powers to extend and preserve life at his command; resurrecting a flat lined patient whose spirit has departed and returning it to the physical body?

Philippians 4:13

I can do all things through him who strengthens me.

I would like to switch our focus to individuals who have claimed to have near death experiences. During the experience, many individuals have claimed to be looking down on their physical body. They then go on to tell how they see light that is so magnificent and peaceful they are drawn to it. In many of these reports, they encounter the voice of a being giving them the choice to stay or go. Many of them also receive a message that they still have a purpose here in the physical world and are returned until a later time. Many psychologists and physicians have defined these experiences as a hallucination comparing the experience to one of a patient who is in a coma. The problem lies in the fact that when we are in a coma, we are in a sleeping state, but when these patient's report the experience, it is at a time when they are flat line and the spark of life has ceased. At this moment in time, there should not be any sign of conscious awareness. The brain is not receiving blood therefore it could not have any sign of activity.

I believe that our conscious awareness does not come from the physical aspect of the brain, but in the spiritual one containing the soul of a person. This awareness is not connected to the body, but a higher power feeding us information, knowledge, wisdom, and messages that we are only able to decipher when we turn to him. Is our consciousness the connection to the higher power? Does it allow us the ability to connect and find understanding once we separate ourselves from the physical things of this world?

In many studies it has been shown during a state of prayer, the brain waves change. Please read the following research article taken from the Psychology in the News website.

http://intro2psych.wordpress.com/2008/03/11/and-this-is-your-brain-on-prayers/

March 11, 2008

... And this is your brain on prayers

Filed under: **brain wiring, evolution, social influence** —

Tags: **meditation, OOA, orientation association area, prayer, religion, SPECT** — intro2psych @ 11:37 am

By Brian Butterworth

From anthropological and historical studies to anecdotal observations, it is not difficult to deduce that religion is an omnipresent characteristic of human society, stretching from the urban centers of countries with over a billion citizens to the most remote islands scattered throughout the world's vast oceans. In sum there are over 10,000 different religions across the planet and just over 5 billion people claim to adhere to one of these vast assortments of spiritual faith. A great deal of scholarship on religion has tended to focus on the social components of religious activity and ceremony, surmising that the community is the driving force behind religion, and that religion existed mostly to serve social functions. However, in recent years neurological scientists have begun to exam the phenomenon of religion in a much more personal context. In an effort to explain the presence religion in human society, a leading neuroscientist, **Andrew Newberg, M.D.**, and his late colleague Eugene D'Aquili, M.D. from the University of Pennsylvania, **studied the brains of monks during meditation** and nuns during intense prayer sessions. What they found was quite remarkable. Doctors Newberg and D'Aquili injected subjects with a radioactive substance and then monitored brain activity with Single Photon-Emission Computed Tomography, or SPECT, a device similar to CAT and PET scan machines. They discovered that certain parts of the brain experience altered levels of activity during religious prayer or meditation. The two observed a decreased level of activity particularly in the orientation association area (OAA) of the brain, the part of the brain responsible for enabling people to distinguish between themselves and objects in the outside world. For D'Aquili and Newburg this indicates a "that spiritual experience, at its very root, is intimately interwoven with human biology. That biology, in some way, compels the spiritual urge." Or as others have put it, human brains are wired for God.

These findings put an interesting twist on the debate over the existence of god, or any greater spiritual being. Many people have cited these findings as evidence that god created humans to be able to relate to God in some way. However such a discovery that suggests we may be biologically engineered for religion poses scientists with provocative questions about why the human brain has evolved in this manner, and what selective advantage this attribute may have provided.

On the other hand, the advantages of human interaction

and cooperation are obvious and can help explain human attachments such as love and friendship. Therefore, from an evolutionary standpoint humans have developed as naturally social creatures, requiring interaction with other humans in order to fully develop psychologically. Understanding a basic human drive to interact with and bond to other humans provides an important baseline for trying to comprehend humans' biological predisposition towards religion. Hans Morgenthau in his book The Restoration of American Politics also recognized the fundamental human yearning to unite with others. He views the impetus for both relationships of love and power to be the result of an existential human feeling of loneliness and the drive to overcome this natural state of separation. In the end, he ultimately concludes that man's goal of unity is frustrated by the inescapable fact that two cannot become one in mind or body (Morgenthau, 1962).

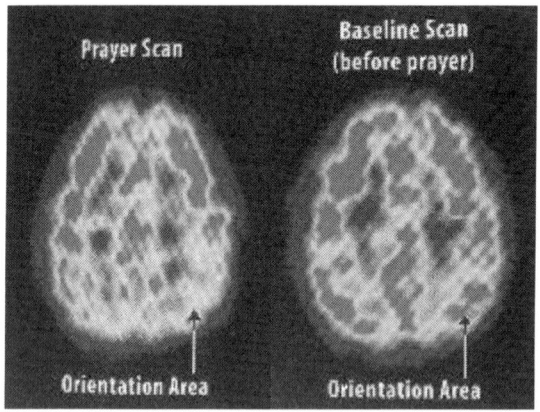

I REST MY CASE!

Chapter 7

What Does the Bible Say About Other

Now we will begin to look at other paranormal phenomena found in the bible.

Psychics/Divination/Necromancy

Leviticus 20:6

"If a person turns to mediums and necromancers, whoring after them, I will set my face against that person and will cut him off from among his people.

Leviticus 20:27

"A man or a woman who is a medium or a necromancer shall surely be put to death. They shall be stoned with stones; their blood shall be upon them."

Leviticus 19:31

"Do not turn to mediums or necromancers; do not seek them out, and so make yourselves unclean by them: I am the Lord your God.

1 Chronicles 10:13-14

...aul died for his breach of faith. He broke faith with the Lord in that he did not keep the command of the Lord, and also consulted a medium, seeking guidance. He did not seek guidance from the Lord.

1 Samuel 28:11-15

Then the woman asked, "Whom shall I bring up for you?" "Bring up Samuel" he said. When the woman saw Samuel, she cried out at the top of her voice and said to Saul, "Why have you deceived me? You are Saul!" The king said to her, "Don't be afraid. What do you see?" The women said, "I see a spirit coming up out of the ground."

Deuteronomy 18:10-12

There shall not be found among you anyone who burns his son or his daughter as an offering, anyone who practices divination or tells fortunes or interprets omens, or a sorcerer or a charmer or a medium or a necromancer or one who inquires of the dead, for whoever does these things is an abomination to the Lord. And because of these abominations the Lord your God is driving them out before you.

Ezekiel 13:6-7

They have seen false visions and lying divinations. They say, 'Declares the Lord,' when the Lord has not sent them, and yet they expect him to fulfil their word. Have you not seen a false vision and uttered a lying divination, whenever you have said, 'Declares the Lord,' although I have not spoken?"

I believe these verses speak for themselves. There is not one instance where it is stated in the bible that it is ok to contact a medium or psychic in order to communicate with a deceased loved one. In fact, it is clearly stated that if you do, you will be deceived by them and this is an abomination to God. They themselves are being deceived by false visions and lying divinations.

We will now look at visions and dreams mentioned in the biblical text.

Visions and Dreams

Joel 2:28

"And it shall come to pass afterward, that I will pour out my Spirit on all flesh; your sons and your daughters shall prophesy, your old men shall dream dreams, and your young men shall see visions.

Daniel 1:17

As for these four youths, God gave them learning and skill in all literature and wisdom, and Daniel had understanding in all visions and dreams.

Numbers 12:6-8

And he said, "Hear my words: If there is a prophet among you, I the Lord make myself known to him in a vision; I speak with him in a dream. Not so with my servant Moses. He is faithful in all my house. With him I speak mouth to mouth, clearly, and not in riddles, and he beholds the form of the Lord. Why then were you not afraid to speak against my servant Moses?"

Acts 2:16-21

But this is what was uttered through the prophet Joel: "'And in the last days it shall be, God declares, that I will pour out my Spirit on all flesh, and your sons and your daughters shall prophesy, and your young men shall see visions, and your old men shall dream dreams; even on my male servants and female servants in those days I will pour out my Spirit, and they shall prophesy. And I will show wonders in the heavens above and signs on the earth below, blood, and fire, and vapor of smoke; the sun shall be turned to darkness and the moon to blood, before the day of the Lord comes, the great and magnificent day....

Daniel 7:1-28

In the first year of Belshazzar king of Babylon, Daniel saw a dream and visions of his head as he lay in his bed. Then he wrote down the dream and told the sum of the matter. Daniel declared, "I saw in my vision by night, and behold, the four winds of heaven were stirring up the great sea. And four great beasts came up out of the sea, different from one another. The first was like a lion and had eagles' wings. Then as I looked its wings were plucked off, and it was lifted up from the ground and made to stand on two feet like a man, and the mind of a man was given to it. And behold, another beast, a second one, like a bear. It was raised up on one side. It had three ribs in its mouth between its teeth; and it was told, 'Arise, devour much flesh ...

Ecclesiastes 5:7

For when dreams increase and words grow many, there is vanity; but God is the one you must fear.

Genesis 37:8

His brothers said to him, "Are you indeed to reign over us? Or are you indeed to rule over us?" So they hated him even more for his dreams and for his words.

Acts 18:9-10

And the Lord said to Paul one night in a vision, "Do not be afraid, but go on speaking and do not be silent, for I am with you, and no one will attack you to harm you, for I have many in this city who are my people."

Acts 16:9

And a vision appeared to Paul in the night: a man of Macedonia was standing there, urging him and saying, "Come over to Macedonia and help us."

Matthew 27:19

Besides, while he was sitting on the judgment seat, his wife sent word to him, "Have nothing to do with that righteous man, for I have suffered much because of him today in a dream."

Hosea 12:10

I spoke to the prophets; it was I who multiplied visions, and through the prophets gave parables.

Daniel 5:12

Because an excellent spirit, knowledge, and understanding to interpret dreams, explain riddles, and solve problems were found in this Daniel, whom the king named Belteshazzar. Now let Daniel be called, and he will show the interpretation."

Daniel 2:28

But there is a God in heaven who reveals mysteries, and he has made known to King Nebuchadnezzar what will be in the latter days. Your dream and the visions of your head as you lay in bed are these:

Daniel 2:16

And Daniel went in and requested the king to appoint him a time that he might show the interpretation to the king.

Job 4:13

Amid thoughts from visions of the night, when deep sleep falls on men

Genesis 41:12

A young Hebrew was there with us, a servant of the captain of the guard. When we told him, he interpreted our dreams to us, giving an interpretation to each man according to his dream.

Genesis 40:8

They said to him, "We have had dreams, and there is no one to interpret them." And Joseph said to them, "Do not interpretations belong to God? Please tell them to me."

Genesis 37:5

Now Joseph had a dream, and when he told it to his brothers they hated him even more.

Although, I have listed many verses here in reference to visions and dreams, these are just a few. There are multiple verses referring to these very same situations. Each time the message is delivered from God or one of his angels as a messenger. Dreams and visions can also be the work of demons. This can manifest itself in nightmares, or deceiving spirits in the case of apparitions, shadow figures, etc.

Angels

Acts 8:26

Now an angel of the Lord said to Philip, "Rise and go toward the south to the road that goes down from Jerusalem to Gaza." This is a desert place.

Acts 10:3

About the ninth hour of the day he saw clearly in a vision an angel of God come in and say to him, "Cornelius."

Acts 12:5-10

So Peter was kept in prison, but earnest prayer for him was made to God by the church. Now when Herod was about to bring him out, on that very night, Peter was sleeping between two soldiers, bound with two chains, and sentries before the door were guarding the prison. And behold, an angel of the Lord stood next to him, and a light shone in the cell. He struck Peter on the side and woke him, saying, "Get up quickly." And the chains fell off his hands. And the angel said to him, "Dress yourself and put on your sandals." And he did so. And he said to him, "Wrap your cloak around you and follow me." And he went out and followed him. He did not know that what was being done by the angel was real, but thought he was seeing a vision

Luke 22:43

And there appeared to him an angel from heaven, strengthening him.

Hebrew 13:1-2

Let brotherly love continue. Do not neglect to show hospitality to strangers, for thereby some have entertained angels unawares.

Luke 1:26-38

In the sixth month the angel Gabriel was sent from God to a city of Galilee named Nazareth, to a virgin betrothed to a man whose name was Joseph, of the house of David. And the virgin's name was Mary. And he came to her and said, "Greetings, O favored one, the Lord is with you!" But she was greatly troubled at the saying, and tried to discern what sort of greeting this might be. And the angel said to her, "Do not be afraid, Mary, for you have found favor with God

In these verses, we can see that God uses his angels as messengers to deliver his word to them. Sometimes they appear as visions or apparitions, and other times they appear in the form of a human. These angels are used to spread God's message and assist God's people. There are also fallen angels, who like the deceiving spirits/demons can perform the same miraculous messages in order to lead God's people astray.

Demons/Familiar Spirits/Deceiving Spirits/Fallen Angels

Matthew 12:43-45

"When the unclean spirit has gone out of a person, it passes through waterless places seeking rest, but finds none. Then it says, 'I will return to my house from which I came.' And when it comes, it finds the house empty, swept, and put in order. Then it goes and brings with it seven other spirits more evil than itself, and they enter and dwell there, and the last state of that person is worse than the first. So also will it be with this evil generation."

Ephesians 6:11-12

Put on the whole armor of God, that you may be able to stand against the schemes of the devil. For we do not wrestle against flesh and blood, but against the rulers, against the authorities, against the cosmic powers over this present darkness, against the spiritual forces of evil in the heavenly places.

Matthew 9:32

As they were going away, behold, a demon-oppressed man who was mute was brought to him.

Luke 9:37-42

On the next day, when they had come down from the mountain, a great crowd met him. And behold, a man from the crowd cried out, "Teacher, I beg you to look at my son, for he is my only child. And behold, a spirit seizes him, and he suddenly cries out. It convulses him so that he foams at the mouth, and shatters him, and will hardly leave him. And I begged your disciples to cast it out, but they could not." Jesus answered, "O faithless and twisted generation, how long am I to be with you and bear with you? Bring your son here."...

1 Kings 22:21-23

Then a spirit came forward and stood before the Lord, saying, 'I will entice him.' And the Lord said to him, 'By what means?' And he said, 'I will go out, and will be a lying spirit in the mouth of all his prophets.' And he said, 'You are to entice him, and you shall succeed; go out and do so.' Now therefore behold, the Lord has put a lying spirit in the mouth of all these your prophets; the Lord has declared disaster for you."

1 Timothy 4:1

Now the Spirit expressly says that in later times some will depart from the faith by devoting themselves to deceitful spirits and teachings of demons

John 10:20

Many of them said, "He has a demon, and is insane; why listen to him?"

Hebrews1:14

Are they not all ministering spirits sent out to serve for the sake of those who are to inherit salvation?

These verses make very clear, the demons are trying to deceive us. They do this in many ways. It can be through causing harm or by simply deceiving others by taking on the role of something familiar. Just as God can choose to show a loved one to deliver a message of peace and hope, Satan and his demons also have the power to take on the physical characteristics of your loved one. By doing this, they too can deceive you and lead you to try and communicate with them.

Casting Out Demons

Matthew 10:1

He called his twelve disciples to him and gave them authority to drive out evil spirits and to heal every disease and sickness.

Luke 10:17

The seventy-two returned with joy, saying, "Lord, even the demons are subject to us in your name!"

Matthew 9:33

And when the demon had been cast out, the mute man spoke. And the crowds marveled, saying, "Never was anything like this seen in Israel."

Matthew 8:16

That evening they brought to him many who were oppressed by demons, and he cast out the spirits with a word and healed all who were sick.

Acts 5:16

The people also gathered from the towns around Jerusalem, bringing the sick and those afflicted with unclean spirits, and they were all healed.

Zechariah 13:2

"And on that day, declares the Lord of hosts, I will cut off the names of the idols from the land, so that they shall be remembered no more. And also I will remove from the land the prophets and the spirit of uncleanness.

Matthew 9:29

And he said to them, "This kind cannot be driven out by anything but prayer."

James 4:7

Submit yourselves therefore to God. Resist the devil, and he will flee from you.

Matthew 25:41

"Then he will say to those on his left, 'Depart from me, you cursed, into the eternal fire prepared for the devil and his angels.

Mark 16:9

Now when he rose early on the first day of the week, he appeared first to Mary Magdalene, from whom he had cast out seven demons.

Where Demons Come From

Ezekiel 13:20

"Therefore thus says the Lord God: Behold, I am against your magic bands with which you hunt the souls like birds, and I will tear them from your arms, and I will let the souls whom you hunt go free, the souls like birds.

Deuteronomy 32:17

They sacrificed to demons that were no gods, to gods they had never known, to new gods that had come recently, whom your fathers had never dreaded.

Psalm 106.37

They sacrificed their sons and their daughters to the demons

Jude 1:6

And the angels who did not stay within their own position of authority, but left their proper dwelling, he has kept in eternal chains under gloomy darkness until the judgment of the great day –

1 Corinthians 10:20

No, I imply that what pagans sacrifice they offer to demons and not to God. I do not want you to be participants with demons.

Leviticus 17:7

So they shall no more sacrifice their sacrifices to goat demons, after whom they whore. This shall be a statute forever for them throughout their generations.

If we look closely at these verses, we are being told that demons come forth when people sacrifice to them and seek them out. The bible tells us that Satan is capable of great miracles. He has powers and the ability to perform many of the same miraculous wonders as God himself. He tries to mimic God's actions to deceive the multitudes of people. These demons are in fact Satan's followers. They have been bound to the earth to wreak havoc on us and try to lead us away from the truths. During those times, the ceremonies and sacrifices offered to demons led to bringing up these harmful spirits. From what we have been shown, seeking out your loved ones will only result in bringing forth these demons who will try to make you believe, you are speaking to your loved one.

Haunted Locations

Job 7:10

He returns no more to his house, nor does his place know him anymore.

Revelation 18:2

And he called out with a mighty voice, "Fallen, fallen is Babylon the great! She has become a dwelling place for demons, a haunt for every unclean spirit, a haunt for every unclean bird, a haunt for every unclean and detestable beast.

In these verses we are being told, there is never a time when a loved one returns to their home. The only time a location is haunted is when it is taken over by familiar spirits/demons who are aware of these same historical facts related to the location. When we go into a location armed with this tragic, historical knowledge and use it to communicate, we are only bringing forth deceitful demons who will make us believe we are speaking to the individuals involved in the tragedy. This will draw you in further to ask more questions and you will be led astray.

Shadow Figures

2 Peter 2:4

For if God did not spare angels when they sinned, but cast them into hell and committed them to chains of gloomy darkness to be kept until the judgment;

James 1:17

Every good gift and every perfect gift is from above, coming down from the Father of lights with whom there is no variation or shadow due to change.

Psalm 23:4

Even though I walk through the valley of the shadow of death, I will fear no evil, for you are with me; your rod and your staff, they comfort me.

Though these verses do not speak directly to shadow figures, the only time a dark shadow is reported in the biblical text is in reference to death or evil. We can come to the conclusion from this, these dark entities are not of God.

Object Manipulation/Electrical Malfunctions

There are no specific verses in the biblical text regarding these phenomenon. However, we know that during the time the bible was written there was no such thing as electricity. We know that in demonic cases, these powerful spirits do have the ability to wreak havoc by manipulating and physically harming things in the environment.

Visible Orbs of Light

Visible orbs of light have been reported by many individuals during near death experiences as well as in many other circumstances. The bible does not specifically speak of orbs of light, but it does reference light associated with God and his angels. In many visions, this illuminating light has documented in the biblical text. We also know that Satan can masquerade as the God of light.

Ghost Hunting

1 Corinthians 10:21

You cannot drink the cup of the Lord and the cup of demons. You cannot partake of the table of the Lord and the table of demons.

Ezekiel 13:18

And say, Thus says the Lord God: Woe to the women who sew magic bands upon all wrists, and make veils for the heads of persons of every stature, in the hunt for souls! Will you hunt down souls belonging to my people and keep your own souls alive?

Though, I have listed many verses in this chapter referring to other paranormal phenomenon, this is barely scratching the surface. We can find answers to each of these questions all in the same source. If you would like to research further the abundance of information available in the bible that you may not have known was there, use the following source. This is a very useful tool for searching any question you may have. Whether it be about the paranormal, relationships, or anything else affecting your life, type your question in the search box and watch all of the information begin to reveal itself. Let this be the source that leads you to your answers.

http://www.openbible.info/topics/

In the next chapter, we will begin to analyze these verses and find truth in each of these experiences.

Chapter 8

Analyzing the Information

In the last three chapters, I have shown you that the bible does in fact speak of many different paranormal phenomena. For some of you, these verses may still be unclear as to the nature of your own experiences. For others who have not had a paranormal experience, I hope I have shown you that ghosts do in fact exist and they are separate from demons. Now let us switch our focus to searching the deeper meanings behind these verses. As we have already learned, sometimes what is right in front of us we cannot see.

In chapters 5 & 7, we spoke about the differences between ghosts, demons, and angels. These verses show us that there are occasions where the spirit of someone who had passed away was seen and shown to others in order to deliver a message. However, if we look at these passages closely, what we do not see is anyone other than Jesus, or the chosen ones of

God returning as a ghost. There is the exception of Samuel. I will show you why I believe this particular instance fits into another category shortly. In some instances, God chose individuals to be resurrected to life in order to show his power and ability. The message is very clear that only he or those he gives authority too can resurrect the dead to life. We are told that Christ and the saints were given eternal life as well as a few others. There is no other mention of an individual soul or ghost appearing in the biblical text. This would lead us to believe that only in certain cases would this be allowed. For those of you who have experienced seeing a loved one after their death, it is very possible that for that moment, God allowed this vision to deliver a message of comfort to you. It is also quite possible that it was a message being delivered by an angelic being transformed into a familiar non-threatening form. We have also noted in some cases, where these spirits could take on the form of another. Angelic beings have this ability in many instances throughout the biblical text.

We are told when we die, that our bodies return to dust and we no longer have any dealings with the living. We are also told in these same verses, we are asleep until the day of return and judgment. This is contrary to popular belief that we go immediately to be with God. We are told in verse after verse that we are asleep and no one ascends to the father except he who descended, Christ himself. This is further verification that Elijah is not with God yet either and possibly did face the first death, but would never see the second. It is also possible that he has been placed somewhere else until the proper time when he is to return to the earth.

We have discussed the possibilities of what happens when we die and where we go until the proper time we are to be raised. There is no doubt we go somewhere after all we have seen, however, we are specifically told that we do not go to be with God until the appointed time. It is also plainly stated, we do not have any part in the affairs of the living.

Now, let's turn our focus to Saul. In the case of Samuel, we must look at this from the entire message that is being given to us. In the verse previous to this one, we are told that God turns away from Saul. At this point, Saul seeks out a medium to find these answers. It is very unlikely that God would allow a medium to give this message when he himself would not. Based on the verses I have provided, there is never an instance where seeking a medium is allowed. In this case, I believe a familiar spirit/demon was brought up through the medium in order to deceive them both. We are told in the following verses that Saul is in fact put to death for going away from God.

We are warned over and over again to refrain from seeking out mediums or psychics, because you will become unclean by them. This does not mean that people do not have gifts, it does mean that they are using them for the wrong purpose. We are told not to seek the dead and using a medium to communicate with them will only bring deception and confusion. How you can analyze this is by seeing what they are using the gift for. There have been many reported cases of police departments utilizing psychics to solve missing person cases. When used in this way, they are not trying to contact or communicate with the dead, but assist in bringing closure and justice. How we know and can test this is if it is being used for the common good, as stated below.

1 Corinthians 12:7

Now to each one the manifestation of the Spirit is given for the common good.

Next, there are those who have experienced visions and dreams. This was a common occurrence in the biblical text when one would seek answers from God. He revealed the mysteries to them through visions, dreams, and the ability to interpret them. He also used other individuals and spiritual powers to deliver these messages as well. In each case to reveal his word to those who could profess and teach it to others. These visions were also witnessed by many so they would know the truth.

These same visions can be given falsely by deceiving spirits to lead you astray. This is where one would say they have encountered an apparition, shadows, visible orbs of light, etc. For those who investigate the paranormal field, wouldn't you agree that these apparitions tend to be attached to a location associated with a tragedy?

As many people believe, there are certain locations that tend to be more haunted than others. Is this really someone being made to relive the tragedy again and again based on what we have learned, or could it be possible that these deceiving spirits would also know the history of the location and use it to their advantage to draw you in further? When speaking of those who have passed, we are told in

Job 7:10

He returns no more to his house, nor does his place know him anymore".

We are also told that the only time a location is haunted is in the case of Babylon the great.

Revelation 18:2

And he called out with a mighty voice, "Fallen, fallen is Babylon the great! She has become a dwelling place for demons, a haunt for every unclean spirit, a haunt for every unclean bird, a haunt for every unclean and detestable beast.

Now let's go back to the ancient beliefs of how this all started. From the earliest of civilizations, people have reported spirits and being frightened of them. If we look at the biblical verses closely as well as the ancient beliefs, a pattern seems to emerge.

In the ancient times people were using sorcery, magic, and sacrifices as well as many other practices in worship to their deceased ancestors. They would give offerings and hold elaborate ceremonies in honor of them. We are also told that they referred to them as God's. In Genesis 6:4, we are told of the Nephilim who were here before and after the flood. These giants were the product of mating between the Sons of God and daughters of men. The evil produced would lead to the great flood to wipe out mankind. We know in the times of ancestor worship and most of the early cultures the worship of multiple God's was a common practice. If these individuals believed they were actual descendants of these God's they would turn to worshiping their ancestors who were partially divine.

Through this sorcery, they were causing demons to be released not only upon themselves, but others around them. These demons originated from the fallen angels who mated with women in Genesis 6:4 producing evil offspring. Later, these descendants began communicating and worshiping them as if they were God. All of their practices were evil and though they were bound in gloomy darkness; as followers of Satan, they too have the ability to come back as these demons and deceive us. We have to remember they too are angels having the abilities that the angels of God also have. We know that Satan has power close to equal to God's and he could perform false miracles in order to counteract God's work. These things were feared then as they are now.

Today, more and more people are reporting having paranormal experiences. The topic has become one of entertainment and excitement. Is it possible that we ourselves are disturbing and raising these restless spirits based on our curiosity to search the other side? Is this why today, more and more people are coming forward and having experiences who have never had them in the past? Are we causing these souls who are supposed to be at rest to relive the very tragic deaths they endured here on earth by using the knowledge of it to contact them? Is that why today, people are becoming more and more drawn to the paranormal and every television channel you turn on has a mystery? Is this why certain buildings are said to be haunted? Is this why we are told not to talk to the dead?

This began in the beginning when we were taught magic arts by those who knew these secrets. Ghosts were not supposed to have any part of the living. They were not supposed to be contacted, but asleep until the Day of Judgment. Resurrecting the souls of ancestors began in the times of the Sumerians and Egyptians. This is why we see reports of them from antiquity, always causing fear. We ourselves may be responsible for the evils in this world. It may be our actions that are afflicting those who don't look into these matters with these spiritual struggles.

Ephesians 6:11-12

Put on the whole armor of God, that you may be able to stand against the schemes of the devil. For we do not wrestle against flesh and blood, but against the rulers, against the authorities, against the cosmic powers over this present darkness, against the spiritual forces of evil in the heavenly places.

So how do we know if what we are experiencing is from God? Have you seen visions, dreams, ghosts, etc.? There is only one way to find the truth in your own experiences.

1 John 4:1-3

Dear friends, do not believe every spirit, but test the spirits to see whether they are from God, because many false prophets have gone out into the world. This is how you can recognize the Spirit of God: Every spirit that acknowledges that Jesus Christ has come in the flesh is from God, but every spirit that does not acknowledge Jesus is not from God.

1 Thessalonians 5:19-22

Do not quench the Spirit. Do not despise prophecies, but test everything; hold fast what is good. Abstain from every form of evil.

Testing Checklist

- ✓ **Did it lead you to God?**
- ✓ **Did it speak of God?**
- ✓ **Did you seek God for the answer?**
- ✓ **Did you test both sides?**
- ✓ **Is it for the common good?**

By using this checklist, searching in the bible, or using http://www.openbible.info/topics/ to find the answer, you can begin to decipher the message and know if it is God, his angels, or Satan at work. The following table summarizes paranormal reports and the categories they fall under.

Demons	Angels	Ghosts
Shadow figures	Voices	Voices
Electrical malfunctions	Orbs of light	Apparitions
Object Manipulation	Apparitions	Visions
Voices	Visions	
Footsteps	Dreams	
Apparition	Take Other Forms	
Visions		
Haunted locations		
Dreams		
Familiar spirits		
Take Other Forms		

What this table shows us is many of our reported experiences can come from every source. The only way to decipher is to test the nature of the experience using the tools I have provided to you. Isn't it apparent that Satan takes the lead in these reported phenomena? We have proven that these experiences can be good or evil. Test them to see if they are from God. Ask yourself the following questions.

Does it lead you to God for answers or away from him? Does it bring understanding or confusion? I urge everyone interested in searching into the paranormal realm to first go to God for these answers and let him lead you to the supernatural truths behind it. Do not search in a one word responses from a ghost box, but in the biblical book of secrets that can answer the whole question.

For those of you who are being negatively affected by these demons, there is only one way to rid yourself of them. A paranormal investigator cannot get rid of them.

Matthew 9:29

And he said to them, "This kind cannot be driven out by anything but prayer."

James 4:7

Submit yourselves therefore to God. Resist the devil, and he will flee from you.

What I have seen and experienced since childhood has not been the ghost of someone familiar. What I have experienced are not the souls of those who have passed into a restful sleep. What I have experienced has been visions and messages that I could not decipher until I began asking God for the answers to them. Much of the fear and misunderstanding came from my own doing, by choosing to seek these answers in the paranormal. By allowing others to tell me where these answers could not be found, it set me on a path away from where I found them. It was when I went to his word for answers that it all became very clear. The very place, I allowed others to tell me, I wouldn't find it.

Chapter 9

Revelations and Consequences

I told you in the previous chapters, there are consequences for seeking this knowledge outside of the appropriate source. By allowing other individuals to influence my belief and understanding of my own experiences, I accepted that this information would not be found in the bible, and took a path to seek the answers in paranormal investigation.

As, I have stated before, the investigations provided another view on the subject. Many interpretations of the experiences and evidence began to lead me to different outside sources of information. I have studied most religious texts, ancient texts, historical data, books on the paranormal, cultural belief, and influences.

I have spoken to many individuals on different sides of thought, both believers and unbelievers. I have searched every area to be led in circles about what is truly happening.

At a point when it seemed, I would never find the answers to my questions, I turned to the bible. At that moment, it became very clear to me that, I had been deceived by people and the understanding I set out to find would soon become clear. I now understood the confusion and the uncertainty. I now knew why one question only led me to another.

2 Corinthians 4:4

In their case the god of this world has blinded the minds of the unbelievers, to keep them from seeing the light of the gospel of the glory of Christ, who is the image of God.

It is important to note that until that moment when, I went to God's word for the answers and truly put myself in a position to search and study only his word, the answers would soon reveal themselves. When we search for this knowledge and understanding outside of God, we are left with many contradicting viewpoints. We listen to everyone's varying interpretations never finding the true answers to the questions. We can be easily influenced and think we know only to be deceived and drawn in further.

It was after I found clarification in the bible to the questions I had sought answers to my whole life, something began to happen. This is a warning to believers and unbelievers. Those Christians who believe they cannot be affected by evil forces are mistaken. Isn't it more likely that a person of God will be affected first? For the unbeliever, the deed has already been accomplished to turn others away from God.

Though, there has been many times throughout my life, I questioned God. Somehow, I always knew he was there. I did not always understand the reasons behind my experiences and trials, but knew there was a purpose. I knew that my Grandma put all her faith in God and to her there was no question about his existence.

Have you ever had a sense of knowing? There is nothing to tell you that you are right, but your instincts tell you that you are. Some instinctual force inside you, leading you.

From childhood, sitting in the pew on Sunday morning, I

would listen, but somehow knowing something wasn't quite right. Was this feeling of knowing coming from my own confusion or put there for a reason? I found it very hard to believe and accept, the God I was being told to go to with all of my questions did not contain these answers as well. Would he allow us to experience things there were no answers for, or is it possible, people have confused this due to their own inability to accept and understand the word of God themselves?

Maybe these scotoma's also were keeping the teachers of the word blinded because they themselves had not tried to understand. We can read the words, but are not shown the meanings until we are awarded the ability to decipher it. Ask and you shall receive.

We sometimes think, the answers should be there at the time we ask. I believe God has a reason not to answer sometimes. It does not mean the answers will always be present at the moment we ask. Sometimes, there are other things that have to take place first. Many of the messages given in the bible were presented in riddles. Until each piece of the puzzle, and each part of the experience had played out, the answers would not be found and understood.

As I have told you, for 35 years and prayer after prayer, I was still left with these questions. At the appropriate time, when I was old enough and had experienced enough, the answers were revealed. While I sat reading the bible and being overwhelmed with excitement, I had finally found the answers I sought. It was at that time, I began to experience the other side of things. I had always felt protected until this point in time. What would begin to happen to me next would further explain any unanswered questions I still had on the subject. I will share my next paranormal experiences with you now.

I purchased a building that had paranormal activity in April 2012. I had investigated this site multiple times and it produced a large amount of evidence. I began to get recordings of a child saying Momma. This happened numerous times after I bought the building. Sometimes the voice would show up on the audio recorder, and sometimes it was audible. Knowing the history associated with the location, I began to wonder if a child may have been harmed there and I went into the cellar to dig. I was drawn in. We uncovered an artifact dated to the 1800's.

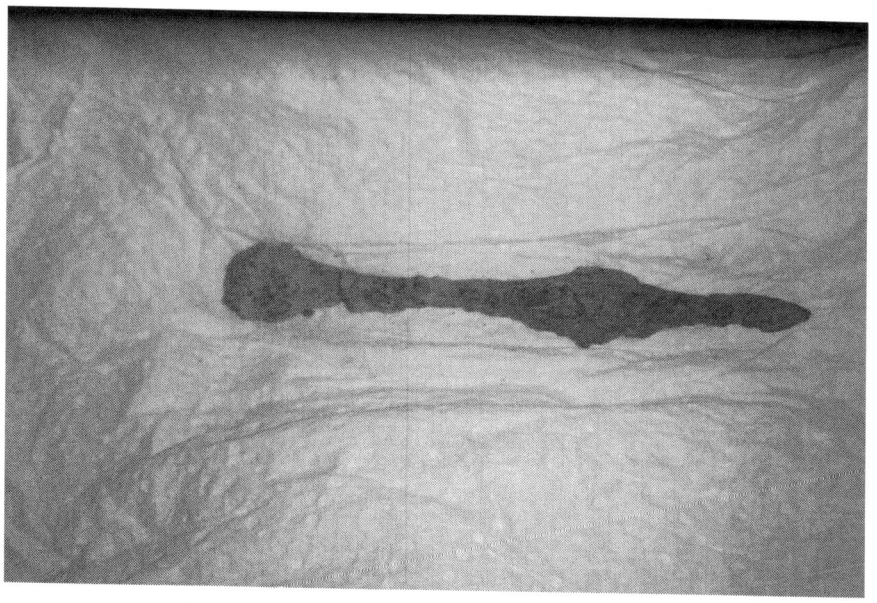

The very same night, while taking pictures in the cellar an image in a mist appeared in one of the photos. It appears to be the head of a grey alien. Now, what I have not told you is,

I captured a recording many years earlier in this same location that was an ancient dead language. I later was led to believe it was Sumerian and began to study those texts as well. The bible also led me to information on these questions about aliens, which will be covered in my next book, "Filling in the Grey Area."

Captured by Markus Avery February 2013

Later that night as we sat in the building, a large hiss came from behind us. We all jumped as it was very loud and disturbing. We left there that night and I brought the artifact home with me.

The day after I found the answers to my paranormal questions in the bible is when all of this would begin to unfold. My choices and actions came with a penalty. Up until this last year, when people have asked me if anything ever followed me home, I have replied no. That all changed when,
I began to uncover these truths through God.

I got up and took a shower. When I stepped out of the shower some writing showed up on the mirror in the steam. Now, originally I thought my kids had done it, but as I looked at it closer, I knew this was not anyone's handwriting in my house. I called my husband in and he too was baffled by it. Two of the words in the message were unclear, while most of it was visible. The writing said, "Tonight I'm gone, xxxxx you so xxxxx." It seemed as though the message was directed at me, but I did not understand the meaning. Later that night, I was getting my grandchild ready for bed. I ran downstairs to get her pajamas and she let out a scream as if she was hurt. I ran upstairs to see what the matter was, but she was no longer standing in the living room. I looked for her and found her under the covers on my bed. I asked her what was wrong and she told me, "I am scared of Big Bird and the baby who shakes his head." She began to shake her head frantically from side to side. This was disturbing like something you would see in a horror film. She was clinging to me and shaking. Since the day she was born, I knew she too was different like me. Strange things happened around her which I captured on video. I calmed her down and got her to bed. I became very upset knowing that something was frightening her.

As, I stood in the kitchen thinking how I did not want her to have the fear that I did as a child, I became very angry. In a loud voice I said, "In the name of Jesus Christ, you are not allowed to scare my grandchild." It was at that moment, I would be hissed at again, this time in my own home.

About an hour later, I remembered the writing on the mirror.

I went in and steamed up the bathroom. I was trying to capture a picture of the writing on the mirror. I took a series of three consecutive photos. In each one something different appeared. I will show you the last two.

Photo 2-In the bottom right corner, a dark shadow begins to form in front of the white door.

Photo 3-In the bottom right corner a solid figure appears. It looks like what my Granddaughter described as a baby. It has one hand holding the counter top.

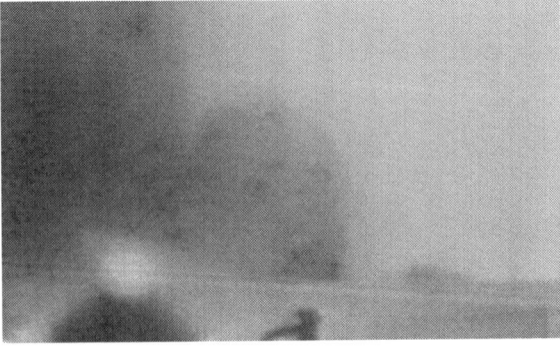

Here is a close up of the same image.

Strange things would begin to happen. My dogs became very protective of me and would try to attack something around me. The fire alarms would go off in succession. I began having nightmares again and losing sleep. I asked God to help me and for a little while my prayer was unanswered. I began to study more in the bible as this was not a figure I could relate to a ghost. It frightened me for my Granddaughter. I began to replay in my mind the order in which these things happened. My Granddaughter would no longer sleep in her room because of Big Bird.

I wondered why after I went to God's word these things were happening to my family. Like a ton of bricks, the understanding came crashing down around me. I had to experience both sides. I had to be tested. The protection that I had always felt left me that night to see the darkness that can affect us. I kept thinking of the message and suddenly it all became clear. "Tonight I'm gone, xxxxx you so xxxxx." I would get the message loud and clear. All of this time, I was searching in the wrong place. I was being protected from these evils that can consume us from a very young age. At a time when I turned to God and was armed with the knowledge of the truths behind these mysteries, I now knew what they were and planned on sharing it with as many people who would listen to me. It was at that moment, my protection left me to see both sides. I was now under attack, though God would not give me more that I could bare.

A series of events began to happen in my life that would help me discern the meaning. I believe this had to happen in order for me to educate others on where these answers could be found. The protection I have always felt left me to see the darkness that we can create. The reward for seeking truth from the correct authority was understanding. I now clearly knew my purpose. I now knew what I had to do. If I had not experienced both sides and tested each view, I would never have understood the true meaning. I now believe my gift is discernment.

Proverbs 16:9

The heart of man plans his way, but the Lord establishes his steps.

I reflected back to the figures I saw that night. I now understood that what I saw was trying to deceive me, trying to keep me off of the path and stumbling into the rock. The very path that God had set for me from the beginning. I had to test every area, I had to experience the confusion and the revelation of truth. If it had not happened just the way it did, I would never have found the answers.

He protected me all through life, knowing that these evils would try to deceive me and confuse my true purpose. On this journey, I have discovered who I am, why I experience things the way I do, and what my true purpose is. I would follow in my Grandma's footsteps, and my Granddaughter will follow in mine.

My purpose is to educate others about the truths behind these experiences. If we never experience or test the dark side, how can we begin to logically explain it to everyone else? In the biblical text, didn't Christ and his disciples also speak to these demons in order to call them out for their true nature and expel them? Who better to lead someone than someone who has studied it and experienced it from both sides? For those who are looking for the answers to their paranormal questions, I can lead them where the true answers lie, back to the very place they also may have been turned away from. For the believer in God who rejects these questions, you can use the same resources to lead them to God.

I have given up the desire to investigate possible haunted locations. I now understand that sometimes what you ask for, may be more than you can handle. Although, I feel I was guided down this path. I will continue to help those who are experiencing these things by leading them to where safety can be achieved. I will continue to research every possible source on unrelated paranormal questions that too can be solved. In order to find the truth we must stick to the facts of the bible, history, etc. Our reality has been created for us through a series of taught belief systems. Follow the evidence that supports the information rather than using theories to justify your position. The word of God tells us what these truths are. Close minded beliefs keep up from seeing reality (gorilla). God is talking, are we listening?

Chapter 10

True Stories of Demonic Possessions

In this chapter, I would like to show you how dangerous demons can actually be. We have all heard of the tales of demonic possession. These are not shown on the news or in the newspapers. You will only find them by searching for the information.

The church has been well aware of these dangers since the beginning of time. The bible tells us of multiple times people were inhabited by demons and cast out. The Church preaches on demons, but fails to discuss the real cases that are affecting God's people today.

The information contained in these stories I will provide are shocking and graphic, but they are very real. The dangers involved in seeking the dead and turning away from God could very well affect you. The following article was taken from the following website.

http://www.oddee.com/item_98653.aspx#LRWf0MvgTT8Rgh4X.99

10 Terrifying Cases of Demonic Possession

7/23/2013 under **Strange Stories** *- by* **Beverly Jenkins**

Though evil spirits possessing the body of a hapless human victim seems like the stuff of science fiction, the possibility of being possessed by demons is, in fact, a common belief held by religions around the world. Even the Christian Bible alludes to demonic possession more than thirty times, including several cases of Jesus "casting out demons" from people. Most religions offer prayers, spells, or incantations that are used to remove these invading spirits via exorcism rituals.

As hard as it may be to believe, countless accounts by victims and witnesses dating back to ancient times are hard to ignore. Let's explore ten cases of truly scary and, by all accounts, real demonic possession.

The Case of Clara Germana Cele

In 1906, Clara Germana Cele was a Christian student at St. Michael's Mission in Natal, South Africa. For some reason, Cele prayed and made a pact with Satan when she was sixteen years-old, and just days later, Cele was overtaken by strange impulses. She was repulsed by religious artifacts like crucifixes, she could speak and understand several languages of which she had no previous knowledge, and she became clairvoyant regarding the thoughts and histories of the people around her.

Nuns who attended to Cele reported that she produced horrible, animalistic sounds; she also levitated up to five feet in the air. Eventually, two priests were brought in to perform an exorcism. Cele tried to strangle one of the priests with his stole, and over one hundred and seventy people witnessed her levitating as the priests read Scripture. Over the course of two days, the rites of exorcism successfully drove the dark spirits from her body.

The Case of Anneliese Michel

Anneliese Michel is a controversial case, as well as the subject of many fictional accounts of her tragic story, most notably the 2005 courtroom drama *The Exorcism of Emily Rose*. Sixteen year-old Anneliese Michel had a history of epilepsy and mental illness, for which she had often been treated at a psychiatric hospital. However, in 1973 Michel become suicidal, spurned all religious artifacts, drank her own urine, and began to hear voices. Medicine did nothing to help the girl, who begged her family to bring in a priest because she believed that she was possessed by demons. Though her request was rejected, two local priests secretly began treating her with exorcism rites. Meanwhile, her parents stopped treating her epilepsy and mental disorders. She was dead within a year.

Michel had almost seventy exorcisms performed on her over the course of ten months. She refused to eat, and often talked of dying as a martyr. Many of the attempted exorcisms were recorded:

Anneliese Michel died from emaciation and starvation. Consequently, her parents and the priests responsible were charged with negligent homicide.

The Case of Roland Doe/Robbie Mannheim

Known as the "real" story behind the novel and Hollywood movie *The Exorcist*, the tale of fourteen year-old Roland Doe is one of the most notorious stories of demonic possession. In fact, Roland Doe is not his real name; it is a pseudonym assigned to him by the Catholic Church in order to preserve the boy's privacy. In the late 1940s, Doe's aunt encouraged him to use a Ouija board, and many speculate that after her death the boy attempted to contact his aunt with the Ouija board, an act which opened the door for the demons who wished to possess him.

The possession started with strange sounds, like dripping water that no one could place. Eventually, religious artifacts began to quake and fly off the walls, and unexplained footsteps and scratching noises could be heard around the home. Scratches began to appear on the boy's body, including words that seemed to have been carved into his flesh by unseen claws. The boy spoke in tongues in a guttural voice and levitated in the air, with his body contorted in pain. His family brought in a Catholic priest, who determined that the boy was possessed by evil spirits and needed an exorcism. The exorcism ritual was performed over thirty times, with the boy injuring the priest many times throughout. When, at last, the rite was successful, the entire hospital heard Doe's cries of bestial anguish and reported a horrible sulfuric odor hanging in the air.

The Case of Julia

In 2008, Dr. Richard E. Gallagher, a board-certified psychiatrist and associate professor of clinical psychiatry at New York Medical College, documented the case of a patient nicknamed "Julia" whom he deduced was indeed possessed by demons. It's rare that a scientist and psychiatrist would acknowledge the possibility of possession; typically doctors think that possession is either fraudulent or a result of mental illness.

Dr. Gallagher personally observed items flying around the room, Julia levitating off the bed, speaking in tongues, and knowing things about people around her that she could not possibly have known. Here is an excerpt from Gallagher's statement:

"Periodically, in our presence, Julia would go into a trance state of a recurring nature," writes Gallagher. "Mentally troubled individuals often 'dissociate,' but Julia's trances were accompanied by an unusual phenomenon: Out of her mouth would come various threats, taunts and scatological language, phrases like 'Leave her alone, you idiot,' 'She's ours,' 'Leave, you imbecile priest,' or just 'Leave.' The tone of this voice differed markedly from Julia's own, and it varied, sometimes sounding guttural and vaguely masculine, at other points high pitched. Most of her comments during these 'trances,' or at the subsequent exorcisms, displayed a marked contempt for anything religious or sacred."

The Case of Arne Cheyenne Johnson

Known as the "Demon Murder Trial," the case of Arne Cheyenne Johnson is the first known court case in the United States during which the defense attempted to prove that the defendant was not guilty by reason of possession.

In 1981, Arne Cheyenne Johnson murdered his landlord, Alan Bono, in Connecticut. Johnson's attorneys argued that his actions indicated a pattern of erratic behavior that had begun when Johnson was just a child. Johnson's family had even consulted with "demonologists" Ed and Lorraine Warren, saying that the child had been taunted and harassed by unknown entities for most of his life. They also asserted that his evil-doings resulted not from a psychological disorder, but from demonic possession.

Ultimately, the judge ruled that demonic possession was not a valid defense against first-degree murder. Johnson was convicted and served a mere five years of his ten to twenty year sentence.

The Case of David Berkowitz, AKA "Son of Sam"

In 1976, the people of New York City were terrorized by a serial killer known as the "Son of Sam," or the ".44 Caliber Killer." For more than a year, the killer lead police on a wild goose chase, leaving behind taunting notes at the crime scenes. Six people were killed and seven others severely wounded in the "Summer of Sam."

When the killer was finally apprehended, he was identified as David Berkowitz. Berkowitz confessed to all of the shootings and claimed that he was commanded to kill by a demon. Berkowitz did not claim to be possessed himself, however; he claimed that his neighbor's dog was possessed, and the dog had ordered him to perform the killings. Berkowitz was sentenced to six life sentences, and in the mid-1990s he issued an amendment to his confession, claiming that he had indeed been a member of a satanic cult that had orchestrated the incidents as part of a ritual murder.

The Case of Michael Taylor

Michael Taylor and his wife, Christine, lived in a small town in Great Britain called Ossett. The couple was very religious, and had joined a Christian prayer group lead by Marie Robinson. At one meeting in 1974, Christine Taylor accused her husband and Robinson of having an affair, which both people hotly denied. Michael Taylor then spewed obscenities and began acting extremely erratic and out of character, leading witnesses to think that he seemed possessed by evil. After months of crazy behavior, Taylor eventually consulted with clergy who performed an exorcism. The exorcism lasted for well over twenty-four hours, and the priests involved claimed to have removed forty demons from the man's body. However, before he left, the priests warned him that the demon of murder remained dormant in his soul.

As soon as Taylor arrived home, he brutally murdered his wife and their dog. He was later found wandering the streets, covered in blood. At his trial, he was acquitted by reason of insanity.

The Case of George Lukins

In 1778, English tailor George Lukins claimed to be possessed. The man would often sing in a voice and language that was not his own, and finally neighbors, concerned by his increasingly frightening behavior, reached out to the church to help the man.

Lukins was sent to a hospital for over twenty months, but doctors could not help him. His caregivers discharged him, even more convinced that his affliction was demonic in nature. During his possession, a very violent Lukins reportedly claimed that he was the devil, barked like a dog, and sang hymns backward. In 1778, after Lukins claimed to be possessed by seven demons that could only be driven out by seven clergymen, the church got involved. Seven priests assembled at Temple Church, where they performed an exorcism. When the ceremony was over, priests claimed that the man had been delivered from the demons who possessed him, and George Lukins exclaimed, "Blessed Jesus!" Lukins then praised God, recited the Lord's Prayer, and thanked the priests.

The Case of Anna Ecklund: The Earling Possession

By the time she was just fourteen years-old, a girl from Earling, Iowa named Anna Ecklund began showing signs of demonic possession. The girl had been raised a devout Catholic, however her father and aunt, who practiced witchcraft, allegedly cursed the girl routinely and used herbs to taint her food. Soon, she could not tolerate religious artifacts, became sexually depraved, and could not enter a church. In 1912, the girl underwent a successful exorcism, but after being "cured" of her possession, her father and aunt prayed to Satan for her to suffer even more, and within a year the girl had become possessed by multiple entities, many of whom are said to be the same spirits who possessed Annaliese Michel.

In 1928, Ecklund again sought help from the church. She was placed in a convent where her exorcism would take place, and the girl's behavior worsened while in the care of the nuns. When the nuns would bless her food before entering her room, Ecklund could sense the blessing. She would hiss at the nuns and throw the food on the floor. She would tolerate food that had not been blessed. Witnesses testified to seeing the girl speak and understand foreign languages she'd never heard before. They also claimed that she defied gravity by levitating and clinging to the wall. The girl was clairvoyant and often vomited and spit at the priests. Her eyes bulged and her body was so bloated and heavy that she nearly broke the iron bed on which she lay.

After twenty-three days and three complete exorcism rituals, the clergymen finally declared her free from the demons who had possessed her.

The Case of Pope Francis Exorcises Boy

The Catholic church performs thousands of exorcisms each year, and Pope Francis has said that he believes that Satan is real, and that the battle against evil is one that he must fight every day. In May of 2013, the newly-elected Pope allegedly performed a brief exorcism live on camera. As he was moving down the line of disabled people, offering blessings, the Pontiff paused before a boy in a wheelchair. Grasping the boy by the head, the boy shuddered and gasped before going limp. (Jenkins, 2013)

There are many other cases of demonic possession on file. Type the words, "True Demonic Possession Cases," in your browsers search engine if you would like to learn more on this topic.

Chapter 11

Why the Church Does Not Talk About It

I would like to begin this chapter by talking about religion. Religion is an organized system of beliefs, ceremonies, and rules used to worship a god or a group of gods. With every religion, there are varying views, practices, and beliefs associated with that particular religion. Each of these religious beliefs, are accepted by its followers. Every day there are new religions popping up everywhere you turn. So, with all of these different religions, how do you know which one is right and which ones wrong? The answer is, all of them and none of them. Each religion only contains a portion of truth, but is it the whole truth and nothing but the truth? I think not.

If you have ever sat down with a group of 100 people and had each person read the same verse of Scripture, you will find that nearly all of them have a different interpretation of what that same verse means. When you find individuals that have similar understanding in their interpretations, these individuals will join together and form denominations. This is how religion is formed. How can it be, if there was only one word of God that we all find different meanings? The answer is, we ourselves are interpreting it. We all think we're right, but we are all truly wrong. We are all blind and ignorant for the most part. This goes back to our accepted beliefs. What we have been taught to believe forces us to try to make every interpretation fit that belief. Does God make the words confusing, or do we confuse the words? God answers the question for us.

2 Peter 1: 20-21

But know this first of all, that no prophecy of Scripture is a matter of one's own interpretation. For no prophecy was ever made by an active human will, but men moved by the Holy Spirit, spoke from God.

So there it is, God does not confuse the meanings, but we

confuse the meanings with our strong beliefs about what the words are saying to us. We try to make every verse fit our own interpretations. By doing this, we find many contradictions between verses within the biblical text. God does not contradict himself. The verses do not contradict the other. With our useless knowledge and lack of understanding, we are blinded to the true meaning of God's word. Until we stop telling everyone this is what it means and start telling everyone read it for yourself, there will always be confusion and contradiction. Only God can reveal the true meaning, but we have to seek it from him only and he will reveal the answer.

Since I was a small child, this has been one of the areas that I've always questioned. Religion itself never made sense to me. I have always felt a higher power, a protective spirit surrounding me, but religious teachings didn't fit my personal experience. I remember being a little kid and asking the question, "What religion was God?" To my amazement, this question was unanswered. Then the next question came. "If God doesn't have a religion, then why do we? " As each question remained unanswered, the next question arose. Have you ever encountered the annoying kid who always asks why? I was that kid.

What I have come to understand is, little children have a better understanding of what the truth is rather than the adults that are teaching them. God is leading them and revealing things to them and people confuse it. They begin to tell you, it's your imagination or you're making it up. Society begins to mold your thoughts, distorting the truths by their own biased opinions until you begin to accept their way of thinking for fear of consequences. This persuasion is a tool used both purposely and without knowing. These scotoma's begin to develop from the moment you begin to communicate. I have now grown into the annoying adult. I still question the interpretations I'm given and I still ask why? Isn't it time that we all started asking why? We are in a time where even church goers are being captured by the entertainment value of these paranormal shows. More and more people are watching and wondering why? Many Christians are now beginning to bring up this topic. Our inability to allow ourselves to step out of the comfort zone and test everything to search for these truths, has left us ignorant and blinded to God's word.

I was talking to a close friend lately, who told me he had asked his pastor why the church doesn't talk about these things. The response he received was "It will cause others to get upset" and "We really don't know the answer".

I myself went to a pastor to try to find meaning for my experiences just a couple of years ago. I thought, I was doing the right thing by seeking these answers from a man of God. From the minute, I said I saw things, he completely shut me down. He would not listen and began to tell me, I was being deceived by demons. When I tried to explain my experiences did not seem to fit into this category, and how I felt the need to find these answers and educate others, I was told I was going to confuse people and would go to hell. Many of us can probably relate to this same experience. It was very upsetting to me. I knew where my heart was and so did God.

My desire to help others understand and my care and concern for other people did not meet the characteristic of evil. The last thing I would ever want to do is deceive anyone. As the religious door slammed in my face, I felt I had no other choice. I would have to search for the answers to these questions on my own.

Why is it that so many churches reject the possibility that some of these experiences are God trying to show us that we don't know it all? Why is it, instead of leading others to the words of God, you are rejected, belittled, and made to feel as if you are evil or there is something wrong with you? There are many of us who are bold enough to ask these questions. There are many more of us that keep the experiences to ourselves for fear of ridicule and accept these secrets will remain hidden. What we do not seem to understand is God does not want us to be confused by the mystery. The answers are all there.

The Church believes in the spiritual realm. They preach from their pulpit about the evils in this world, but do not address the experiences people are having. In my experience, I have not found one pastor who will touch this subject. We know from the teachings there are angels and demons, there are visions and dreams yet, when an experience is brought forward, it is labelled only evil.

Why do our religious beliefs focus primarily on the negative aspect of the spiritual realm? Didn't God tell us, he works miracles and sends us messages the very same way? There are many people who are having just as many positive experiences that they too need answers for. If we can provide them with the knowledge and lead them to the place they can find the answer, we are doing God's will. Rejecting these questions will only lead them further away from God.

2 Corinthians 4:18

So we fix our eyes not on what is seen, but on what is unseen. For what is seen is temporary, but what is unseen is eternal.

It is important for our church leaders today to begin to address these questions; to preach on these topics as they are becoming more and more a daily conversation. If you are avoiding the topic for fear of stirring up controversy, you are not following God's word. If you are avoiding the topic, because you do not have the answers, you are not asking God to lead you to them. Isn't it time that the church starts researching the topic further, so that they can lead their congregation to God's word and not our interpretations of it? These times we are in are frightening. Stop turning people away in the path of further confusion, but to the place you were meant to. Arm yourselves with this knowledge, so that these very questions can be answered. When I look back at what was being done in the time of Noah, I can't help but feel we are repeating the past. It is time we all do the following:

Ephesians 6:11

Put you on the armour of God that you may be able to stand against the deceits of the devil. For our wrestling is not against flesh and blood; but against principalities and power, against the rulers of the world of this darkness, against the spirits of wickedness in the high places.

Couldn't you do the same research I have done? Instead of rejecting people's questions and turning them away from the bible, shouldn't you also be directing them to the very book in your hand that contains these answers?

I ask you next time, will you be the one who leads or follows the false ideals we have come to accept? Lead them to God's word, not yours. Let God's word be the only word you listen to and accept. From the verses I have provided we can come to the following conclusion.

It is God's will to choose when the soul of someone past will present itself to bring a message of peace and hope. Only he allows this message to be sent. Seeking them out or providing an invitation will not lead to seeing or speaking with your loved one. It will lead to contact with forces much more powerful than yourself. By doing this, we can open doors we cannot close.

2 Corinthians 11:14

And no wonder, for Satan himself masquerades as an angel of light.

1 Timothy 4:1

Now the Spirit expressly says that in later times some will depart from the faith by devoting themselves to deceitful spirits and teachings of demons.

Visions and messages are sent to us, but the interpretation lies with God. Do not ask a paranormal investigator to explain it. Do not ask your pastor to interpret it. Do not ask a medium to find the message. Let God interpret it for you. Test the experience by searching for truth and meaning in the appropriate place and it will be revealed to you when the time is right.

Now, I am not ungrateful or being sarcastic when I tell my experiences with the church. If it had not been for these encounters, I would never have followed the path God chose for me. There are many churches who simply don't know how to address this topic. Fear that they themselves may be going against the word of God could possibly be the reason. For those of you who speak to your congregation regarding these topics, I applaud you. It is important to address all of God's words and not just those that fit your beliefs.

I have not given up my research of the secrets God is trying to reveal to me. I will continue to help those experiencing both the positive and negative side of these powerful forces by arming them with the resources to search and find meaning. If we only examine one side, we will always arrive at the same conclusion.

Chapter after chapter of this book, I have shown to you through my experiences and research that God has had a hand in every area. Am I providing you with false teachings or did I speak of God? Did I tell you to reject him or embrace him? Reject every opinion and theory I have given. Test every word. Regardless if I am right or wrong, if it leads you to re-evaluate and read the word of God, you are on the right path to finding your answers.

We are all being tested. The mystery remains due to our inability to seek the answers from the proper source. There is no mystery here. The answers are in plain sight. Your questions will be answered, but not until you go to God.

One person can make a difference, but everyone should try.

~JFK

Chapter 12

What It All Means

What I have come to understand fully is, sin is that which you know is wrong and do intentionally. However, by searching for the answers to my experiences, the intention is to let Gods words guide me and lead me to the truths. From this, I know my intention is pure of heart and not an abomination of God. This was put in my life for a reason, and the road I had to take from a very young age was paved by him. Each step has led me further to the answers and peace. There are times, I have focused on the rock and stumbled only to get up and find my way.

I sat thinking one day about what all this means. As, I look back on the experiences I have had and the journey it has taken me on, I know that God is on my side. I have not always made the right choices. I have not always asked God to lead my way, but he has walked beside me on this path to help me find truth.

In this last chapter, I want to go back to the beginning when we looked at the viewpoints of God exists verses God does not exist.

To the believer, there is no question that God exists. He is influencing every aspect of their life. He gives blessings for leading a Christian life and brings hardship punishing those who live a sinful one. He allows Satan to influence us. Only by praying, repenting, and accepting him will we one day receive eternal life.

To the unbeliever, there could not be a God. What God who is supposed to be so loving would allow for such pain and suffering of those he created? Who would allow innocent children to be molested and animals to be harmed? Why doesn't he show himself or answer our prayers when we ask? Why doesn't he lead us to the truths instead of keeping us confused and questioning everything?

Now after looking at both sides of this, I believe I can say to some extent both views are correct.

To the believer. God is already working in your life. He is leading you to seek knowledge and understanding from him. He is rewarding you for your faith. However, he has also provided you with the ability to test and search everything. There is more to learn, and by seeking you will find peace in the unanswered questions that still remain. Start listening to other beliefs, not accepting them, but testing them to find the truth.

For the unbeliever, we do face a lot of struggles in our lives. There is much wickedness in this world that afflicts all of us. There are times where our prayers go unanswered and the word is confusing. Now let me explain why.

As, I sat in silence one day thinking about the many conflicting views, opposite beliefs, differences in religion, and how there are always two sides to everything; I realized something extraordinary. In every aspect of our lives, there are opposites. Whether it be between good and evil, true or false, life and death, belief or unbelief, positive and negative, etc., there are always two sides. One side of the equation by itself cannot solve the problem. No understanding comes by only looking at one side. Until these two opposing forces come together, neither is powerful alone. It is when they meet that balance is achieved.

One may have asked the question, "How can God be perfect, yet allow such Evil?" Good and evil have been present from the beginning and we began to know the difference too when Adam sinned.

Genesis 3:22

And the Lord God said, "The man has now become like one of us, knowing good and evil.

What this tells us is, these two powerful forces have been present since the beginning. It was not until they came together that balance was achieved. I believe God is that balance and that everything is predetermined. Each of the struggles we face are a learning experience. Each positive experience provides hope. If we did not experience both sides, we would never have anything to learn. We would never test both sides and we would never achieve balance. So, God is not causing these negative afflictions on us. The devil is using his power on the evil side and God is using his on the positive side. Each of these has to take place in order for us to learn. Both sides have to happen so we ourselves can achieve balance. Once we achieve that balance by letting him interpret the meaning, we then find our purpose.

From my own personal experiences in childhood to the present time, I have developed the understanding that our beliefs keep us from reaching our true potential and finding our true purpose. We develop metal blocks that hinder our ability to see beyond what fits our current perception. This is why I believe children and animals are more sensitive to having paranormal experiences. Society has not yet brainwashed them into believing these things are not their reality.

When we begin to let go of our preconceived notions, a whole new world of understanding begins to evolve.

I know someone who has a form of autism. He is one of the most intelligent people I have ever met. He is socially awkward by our standards. I believe what one calls a disability is in fact a blessing in disguise. Because of this labeled disability, he is not subject to the automatic acceptance of what others say. He is not socially influenced by his surroundings, but is locked inside his own world where he is able to critically analyze and question everything.

I believe, this affords him the ability to seek greater knowledge and understanding. This is something most of us cannot do, unless you fall into the category of the 5 percent. Maybe, we would all be better off if we had these same disabilities.

So let me ask you again, are you focusing on the field or the rock? If God is the field and Satan is the rock. Do we continue to listen to others varying interpretations of the truth eventually stumbling and losing our way, or do we focus on the field and let it lead us further and further to reach the expanses of it? Do you choose the reality of endless peace or do you choose to keep hitting the rock never reaching your destination? Will you continue to focus on one side of thought instead of testing both sides to achieve balance? It does not matter how we get there so long as we do. For some that will be through an inner desire to allow God to lead them (spirit) for some a sense of knowing and searching for validation for their truths (wisdom) for some revealing spiritual messages that they have received from a greater power in order to provide education on the truth (prophesy) for some the inner drive to understand their paranormal experience and search within themselves and God for the answers allowing them the ability to know good from bad (discernment). So you see, we are each different. We have different gifts that serve individual purpose. All for the time when they come together for the ultimate ending. I hope this book leads you to reevaluate your beliefs. Allow yourselves to begin your own journey avoiding the rock and focusing on the field. There is only one way to achieve the answers to your questions. Test everything. Test every spirit to know if they are of God, and test your own beliefs to see what brings you peace.

I can only tell you that I believe this knowledge and understanding comes from something much greater than myself. The drive within me has been fed by a powerful spirit leading me to these truths. This journey has been a humbling one. In this case, I believe through the darkness, I found the light.

Now in the final note, let me take you back to the poem I wrote and dedicated to my Grandma in the beginning of this book. Please read this again.

It is not goodbye. It is just so long until we meet again.

Just remember, I'll be here until the very end.

I may be gone, but you should know, I have been here from the start.

And, even though you can't see me, you will feel me in your heart.

It is not goodbye. It is the test of time that strengthens us within.

Until the day that our souls are free to meet up once again.

It is not goodbye, remember me in every moment given.

And, keep with you my promises to be with you in heaven.

While writing my book, "Soul Searching," I told you it had multiple meanings. What I didn't realize was that while typing the pages the meaning would become even clearer to me. Though, I wrote this poem at 12 years old and the words were printed with my hands, as I typed this very last chapter, I realized the message this poem was sending to me. Not only does it hold special to my heart for her, but I realized the same words were being told to me by the very thoughts given to me to write it. Through these words, Christ is telling me the same promise. At a time, when he left me physically, he has always been with me and will be again in heaven.

It is what we don't see that gives us sight

~Chilton 2013

Final Acknowledgement:

Thank you to all believers and nonbelievers who read this book. Thank you to all of you who put your taught and accepted beliefs aside to open your minds to test the information I have provided. Thank you to God for providing me with the strength to face both sides of reality and leading me to balance and peace within my life.

Glossary of Terms

Ancestor worship- the custom of venerating deceased ancestors who are considered still a part of the family and whose spirits are believed to have the power to intervene in the affairs of the living. Ancient- very old: having lived or existed for a very long time: of, coming from, or belonging to a time that was long ago in the past.

Angel- a spiritual being that serves especially as a messenger from God or as a guardian of human beings

Antiquity- ancient times: very great age

Aojha-spirit guide

Ba-the soul

Belief- a feeling of being sure that someone or something exists or that something is true: a feeling that something is good, right, or valuable: a feeling of trust in the worth or ability of someone

Bhoot-supernatural creature, usually the ghost of a deceased person

Bhut- supernatural creature, usually the ghost of a deceased person

Bible- the book of sacred writings used in the Christian religion: the book of sacred writings used in the Jewish religion

Christian- one who professes belief in the teachings of Jesus Christ

Death- the end of life: the time when someone or something dies: the ending of a particular person's life: the permanent end of something that is not alive: the ruin or destruction of something

Deceiving spirits-demon sent to deceive the living and lead them astray into spiritual bondage

Demon- an evil spirit: a person who has a lot of energy or enthusiasm: something that causes a person to have a lot of trouble or unhappiness

Demonic- of, relating to, or suggestive of a demon

Denomination- a religious group with agreed upon beliefs

Divination- the art or practice that seeks to foresee or foretell future events or discover hidden knowledge usually by the interpretation of omens or by the aid of supernatural powers: unusual insight: intuitive perception

Dream- a series of thoughts, visions, or feelings that happen during sleep: an idea or vision that is created in your imagination and that is not real: something that you have wanted very much to do, be, or have for a long time

Evidence-something which shows that something else exists or is true: a visible sign of something

Exorcism-the act or practice of removing demons

Experience-the process of doing and seeing things and of having things happen to you

False prophet-someone or something who speaks blasphemy or lies as if it were true to deceive others

Familiar spirits- a spirit or demon that serves or prompts an individual: the spirit of a dead person invoked by a medium to advise or prophesy

Figurative blind spot- An inability to recognize a fact or think clearly about a certain topic

Ghost- the soul of a dead person thought of as living in an unseen world or as appearing to living people: a very small amount or trace

God- the perfect and all-powerful spirit or being that is worshipped especially by Christians, Jews, and Muslims as the one who created and rules the universe: a spirit or being that has great power, strength, knowledge, etc., and that can affect nature and the lives of people: one of various spirits or beings worshipped in some religions: a person and especially a man who is greatly loved or admired

Healing- to become healthy or well again: to make (someone or something) healthy or well again

Historical- of or relating to history: based on history: arranged in the order that things happened or came to be

Immortal-not capable of dying: living forever

Immortality-the quality or state of someone or something that will never die or be forgotten: the quality or state of being immortal

Insight- the ability to understand people and situations in a very clear way: an understanding of the true nature of something

Intelligent haunting- A haunting in which a spiritual entity is aware of the living world and interacts with or responds to it

Invisible- impossible to see: not visible

Jesus Christ- the highest human corporeal concept of the divine idea rebuking and destroying error and bringing to light man's immortality

Jinn-ghost: spirit

Khu-luminous part of a man: soul: malignant ghost that enters the human body of the living to torture

Knowledge- information, understanding, or skill that you get from experience or education: awareness of something: the state of being aware of something

Likability-having qualities that bring about a favorable regard; pleasant; agreeable

Magic- a power that allows people (such as witches and wizards) to do impossible things by saying special words or performing special actions: tricks that seem to be impossible and that are done by a performer to entertain people: special power, influence, or skill

Medium- used to describe strange mental powers and abilities (such as the ability to predict the future, to know what other people are thinking, or to receive messages from dead people) that cannot be explained by natural laws *of a person* : having strange and unnatural mental abilities : having psychic powers: of or relating to the mind

Mental block- an inability to remember or think of something you normally can do; often caused by emotional tension

Message-a piece of information that is sent or given to someone

Messenger- someone who delivers a message

Near death experience- personal experiences associated with impending death, encompassing multiple possible sensations including detachment from the body, feelings of levitation, total serenity, security, warmth, the experience of absolute dissolution, and the presence of a light

Necromancy-the practice of talking to the spirits of dead people: the use of magic powers especially for evil purposes

Normal-usual or ordinary; not strange

Paranormal-very strange and not able to be explained by what scientists know about nature and the world

Persuasion- the act of causing people to do or believe something: the act or activity of persuading people

Phenomenon- something that can be observed and studied and that typically is unusual or difficult to understand or explain fully: someone or something that is very impressive or popular especially because of an unusual ability or quality

Poltergeist-noisy ghost: physical manifestation created by ones emotional state

Psychic- used to describe strange mental powers and abilities (such as the ability to predict the future, to know what other people are thinking, or to receive messages from dead people) that cannot be explained by natural laws *of a person* : having strange and unnatural mental abilities : having psychic powers: of or relating to the mind

Psychological awareness- the state or quality of being aware of something

Psychology- the science or study of the mind and behavior

Purgatory- a state after death according to Roman Catholic belief in which the souls of people who die are made pure through suffering before going to heaven: a place or state of suffering

Realm- an area of activity, interest, or knowledge

Reincarnation- the idea or belief that people are born again with a different body after death: someone who has been born again with a different body after death

Religion-an organized system of beliefs, ceremonies, and rules used to worship a god or a group of gods

Residual haunting- Repeated playbacks of auditory, visual, olfactory, and other sensory phenomenon that are attributed to a traumatic event, life-altering event, or a routine event of a person or place, like an echo or a replay of a videotape of past events

Resurrection- the rising again to life of all the human dead before the final judgment: the state of one risen from the dead

Scotoma- a figurative blind spot in a person's psychological awareness

Sensory- of or relating to sensation or to the senses

Shiryo- soul of the dead

Sorcery- the use of power gained from the assistance or control of evil spirits especially for divining

Soul- the spiritual part of a person that is believed to give life to the body and in many religions is believed to live forever: a person's deeply felt moral and emotional nature

Spirit- the force within a person that is believed to give the body life, energy, and power: the inner quality or nature of a person

Spiritual death-death of the soul, spirit, or ghost

Spook-phantom: apparition

Supernatural-unable to be explained by science or the laws of nature: of, relating to, or seeming to come from magic, a god, etc.

Traditional haunting- A haunting in which a spiritual entity is aware of the living world and interacts with or responds to it

Visible- able to be seen: easily seen or understood

Vision- the ability to see: sight or eyesight: something that you imagine: a picture that you see in your mind: something that you see or dream especially as part of a religious or supernatural experience

If you liked this book. Please watch for my next book coming out early 2014.

"Filling in the Grey Area"

The Truth about Aliens, Who We Are, Mysterious Secrets Revealed, and What Is yet To Come.

For comments, questions, or sharing information, you can contact me via email at findingtruthseries@live.com

I am also available for book signings, group presentations, and educational seminars.

Sources

Bible, T. (2013). *What Does the Bible Say.* Topical Bible. Retrieved from http://www.openbible.info/topics

Butterworth, B. (2008). Psychology in the News. Retrieved from http://intro2psych.wordpress.com/2008/03/11/and-this-is-your-brain-on-prayers/

Dennis Coon. (2006). *Psychology-A Modular Approach To Mind and Behavior* (Vol. 10). Wadsworth Thomson Learning.

Guiley, R. E. (2007). *The Encyclopedia of Ghosts and Spirits.* New York: Checkmark Books.

Guiley, R. E. (2009). *The Encyclopedia of Demons and Demonology.* New York: Checkmark Books.

Jay P. Green, S. (1984). *The Interlinear Bible Hebrew-Greek-English.* Hendrickson Publishers.

Jenkins, B. (2013). *10 Terrifying Cases of Demonic Possession.* Beverly Jenkins. Retrieved from http://www.oddee.com/item_98653.aspx#LRWf0MvgTT8Rgh4X.99.

Kaczmarek, D. (2009). *Field Guide to Ghost Hunting Techniques.* Ghost Research Society Press.

Ken Johnson, T. (2009). *Ancient Paganism The Scorery of the Fallen Angels.* BibleFacts.Org.

Morgenthau, H. (1962). *The Restoration of American Politics.* Chicago: University of Chicago Press.

NLT, N. N. (1995). *Today's Parallel Bible.* Guideposts.

Simons, D. J. (1999). *Selective Attention Test.* You Tube. Retrieved from http://www.youtube.com/watch?v=vJG698U2Mvo

Unknown. (n.d.). *Description of Examples of Static Electricity.* 2010: Maher Science.

Version, K. J. (1964). *New Analytical Bible and Dictionary of the Bible.* John A. Dickenson Publishing CO.

Version, N. I. (1973). *Holy Bible*. International Bible Society.

Walther, H. (1977). *The Answer Two Raptures*. Prophetic Books, Inc.

Wayne Weiten, M. A. (2009). *Psychology Applied in the Modern Life*. Wadsworth Cengage Learning.

Wikipedia. (2013). *Ghost*. Wikipedia. Retrieved from http://en.wikipedia.org/wiki/Ghost

Wikipedia. (2013). *Near Death Experience*. Wikipedia. Retrieved from www.wikipedia.com/neardeathexperience

Notes

Notes

Notes

Notes

Notes

Notes

Notes

Made in the USA
Charleston, SC
10 December 2013